Celebration of Love

Mary O'Hara
Celebration of Love
A collection of favourite prose and poetry

HODDER AND STOUGHTON
LONDON SYDNEY AUCKLAND TORONTO

British Library Cataloguing in Publication Data

Celebration of love: a collection of favourite
    prose and poetry.
    1. Love——Literary collections   2. English
    literature
    I. O'Hara, Mary, 1935–
    820.8'0354   PR1111.L7

ISBN 0-340-37323-7

Hodder and Stoughton Editorial Office: 47 Bedford Square,
London WC1B 3DP

Be of love a little more
careful than of anything else

Louis Evely

CONTENTS

Preface

Borrowed Plumes

Borrowed Plumes

One of Aesop's fables is about a jackdaw that borrowed peacocks' feathers to make himself appear beautiful – an apt image for a personal collection of other people's thoughts. This book is an anthology of favourite readings about love. It is called *Celebration of Love* because love is intrinsically something celebratory, a form of rejoicing about life.

The word love is bandied about a lot nowadays, mostly with a sexual connotation. Everyone today is much more open about such matters, but when I was a small child that subject was more or less taboo. Embarrassed parents explained the facts of life to their offspring by basing their talk on that well-worn theme of the birds and the bees. This mystique about the birds and the bees prompted in me a fascination with these creatures. Honey is my staple sweetener; my cottage garden is lived in by a variety of birds but with shame I must confess that to this day I don't know how either species reproduce! Perhaps it is no accident then that Brigid Marlin, the illustrator, has chosen birds as a theme for the anthology because she knows of my affection for them and she also points out that the birds and I share the same profession. Brother Bee has a special extract all to himself in the chapter on 'Love and Creation'.

There are of course more aspects of love than the merely sexual or even the romantic one. Love is a much grander thing, much more multifaceted and wider in scope. The mother enfolding the infant in her arms, the friend or family giving selfless support in times of difficulty, the caring for the handicapped and sick in society, Mother Teresa and others like her giving of themselves unstintingly for the poor, the contemplative, of whatever religion, in silent prayer for mankind – all these are superb manifestations of love. Beyond, within and above,

making all that possible, the mighty love of God whose Spirit

> . . . over the bent world broods,
> With warm breast and with ah!
> Bright wings.

Love Himself sustaining life in all its forms from the shining Seraphim to the lowly earthworm.

All things are related to God and to one another in a loving, living chain. This interrelatedness can be felt in the pulse of the variety of life about us. Sometimes, indeed, the contribution of the industrious earthworm in this loving chain is more immediately apparent than that of theological theses. Just as the worm renews the soil by its constant turning and burrowing, so too I would hope that my browsing through other people's writings might turn up fresh and fertile soil for others to benefit from.

My career as a singer affords many opportunities to give and receive love. Each person's appreciation and understanding of love is coloured by personal experience, not only of his or her loving, but also of being loved. For this reason one person's definition of love will vary from the next. But most of us recognise love instinctively when we see it. It is much more pervasive than the news headlines would lead us to believe. One of the things that has helped me most in my personal and professional life is the encouragement and affection I have constantly received from those who have come across my work. How thankful I am for the opportunities I've had in the areas of my work to love and be loved. It so happens that I've been blessed with a happy disposition and, accustomed as I am to looking at life with a benign eye, this probably preconditions my attitude towards people and events. In my own life happy memories predominate and I find little difficulty seeing life as one continuous manifestation of various aspects of love, however veiled it sometimes is. It is glimpses of these various aspects of love that I set out to bring together in this collection.

My autobiography is entitled *The Scent of the Roses,* a phrase culled from a poem by Thomas Moore, a favourite Anglo-Irish poet of the late eighteenth, early nineteenth century. The poem is about love and friendship gratefully remembered, and in the autobiography I wrote extensively about love and its influence in my own life, especially as regards my marriage to Richard Selig. It was the exceptional measure and quality of God-given happiness and love experienced in our marriage that sustained me throughout the period of my husband's illness and premature death and the years that followed. Eventually I was led to abandon singing and embrace the monastic life, and for twelve and a half years I lived a life of silence and prayer as a member of a contemplative community of Benedictine women. If I learnt anything from those silent years and the events that preceded them, it is that love is one, but many faceted. During my monastic sojourn I lived side by side with a large group of other women from a cross-section of society. Many of them were people with whom, in ordinary secular circumstances, I would not have chosen to live and with

whom I would not have had the opportunity to associate. I grew to love them as I believe they grew to love me, and when eventually ill health occasioned my leaving the community, I carried with me their affection for which my life is the richer today.

The business of serious reading did not begin for me until the death of my husband. This habit was further developed while at Stanbrook Abbey. Study, like manual work, is a hallowed part of the Rule of Saint Benedict. Nowadays, reading, like lying flat on the ground, is one of my favourite methods of relaxing, a great release from the more taxing features of my work as a singer. Of course it need hardly be said that reading is also much more than just relaxation. It is nourishment. Now that I have returned to my singing career, travelling frequently by plane and waiting around airports in different parts of the world, there is ample opportunity for reading. As I go along I mark passages that appeal to me, for whatever reason – sometimes because they are well crafted, or simply for their beauty, or because they are witty or because suddenly and unexpectedly they cast a new light on and freshen up what was hitherto a familiar but stale truth. When this book was first suggested my initial reaction was to reread these marked passages in the books on my shelves. Serendipitously, perhaps, I found that many of my favourite pieces fitted into the

publishers' brief.

Every anthology, however eclectic, contains a strong element of the personal. It can illuminate the personality of the selector better than any autobiography. Therefore, whether I like it or not, this collection is a statement about me. In it there has not been a great deal of philosophising about the nature of love. The selected passages do it for me. I tend to believe that love, like truth, is best portrayed in stories – just as action is supposed to speak louder than words.

After *The Scent of the Roses* I put together a book called *A Song for Ireland,* dealing with that part of the musical heritage of my country wherein my work is rooted. This was in a sense an amplification of my autobiography, as is this present book *Celebration of Love*. Just as I was fortunate to have *A Song for Ireland* illustrated by some excellent photographers, so too I'm fortunate here in Brigid Marlin, painter and writer. She is a friend of long standing – since student days in fact when together we attended the College of Art in Dublin.

As in any book of this nature, there comes a stage, when if only for the sake of order, one must sift through the material and divide it into chapters. Some passages proved easy to categorise but others were less so because they were subject to a variety of interpretations. In such cases I just pleased myself. A much more difficult problem,

however, was deciding when to cut, but I comforted myself with the hope that the reader, once the appetite is whetted, will seek out the original. I regard the collection as food for thought – something to be tasted now and again as mood and time permit. It is distilled wisdom, plumes borrowed from other people's finery. Finally, I hope that those who read this book will receive as much pleasure from it as I found in putting it together.

Mary O'Hara

Love
and
Creation

Love and Creation

Morning has broken like the first morning
Blackbird has spoken like the first bird

———————

Whenever I sing those words it strikes me anew that God's act of creation is unbroken. He did not stop creating after the biblical seven days; His act of creating takes place every morning, every instant.

As I sit here writing this, I look out on to my garden; it is late winter and the snowdrops, gentle and brave, are fresh reminders of this joyous truth. Perhaps their very being is a giving back of praise and thanksgiving to their Creator. It's an exciting thought that it is Love Himself who makes to run the same stream of life through the vein of rock and leaf and man; that, linked together in creative love, we are all part of the whole, each with its or his or her role to play, joining hands in the great invisible cosmic dance. Poets and painters who are sensitive to the rhythm of the earth often remark on how their creativity is geared to the earth's seasonal cycle. With the resurgence of Spring they experience their own 'creative sap rising'. An American author wrote to me the other day claiming that she's always had 'a love affair with the wind... I even had a window once which "played" tunes determining how I opened or closed it'. Being an interpretative artist rather than a creative one I do not feel this so strongly, but I am tuned to the earth in my own way.

One of the penalties of being a professional singer is that so often one is cut off from nature for long periods of time through being shut indoors. In many a hotel, I've created unease by asking for a room which has windows that open, only to be told, sorry, the windows are now built not to open. This makes me all the more appreciative of the good moments in travelling, the periods of closer contact with nature, such as a recent afternoon's roaming in a remote wood deep in Western Canada. Having had to beat a hasty retreat to our boat when we smelt and saw the footprints of a grizzly bear and its young merely added a touch of danger and drama to a perfect day's outing. I tour Canada usually in Spring and Autumn and I've found nothing yet to equal the Rocky Mountains when the landscape turns to gold and the leaves begin to fall. On another occasion I relaxed in a hot sulphur pool in Banff, in the foothills of the Rockies, watching the snow falling silently all round and melting in the steam. And then I returned to my sixteenth-century thatched cottage in Berkshire to be greeted by the glorious autumnal chaos of my garden. But soon, after it's had its winter rest, the secretive, exciting things will start happening in the garden and the seasonal miracle will take place once more. Such is creation, the renewal constantly going on all around us, giving us pause and warming the heart afresh. Creation is indeed an ongoing love story.

A LEGEND OF ST FRANCIS

Anon

. . . Now about the time of Christmas I was sent on an errand to the convent of the Sisters, and coming to the place at the time of Vespers I waited without. And those Sisters were singing the Holy Office, wherefore I hearkened to them. So when it came to *Magnificat,* as one sang the Antiphon, there arose a loud and grievous howl. And all my heart melted, for it was the howling of my Brother as he was wont to howl gladly and unchecked at a time of moonlight; only the Brethren could not abide it, but Francis ever loved to hear him give tongue. And I listened as one that dreamed. And all through the holy song of *Magnificat* did Brother Wolf howl unchecked, and that fearful sound was full of joy, and that the Creator heard it so I am sure, for it was the voice of one who has come to that secret joy that lies at the heart of pain, and brings us, whosoever we be, into the secret brotherhood that no man may enter by any other way than the Royal Way of Suffering and Love . . .

So after Vespers was over I heard the glad sound of women's voices, and it seemed to me that they made merry with love in their hearts; and ever and anon I heard the deep growl of him I loved, yea, of him who was loved by Francis and all the gentle and simple.

Now at that time, because my joy at finding Brother Wolf was so deep, I went not in: I hearkened awhile to their joyous voices and departed, giving thanks; for the Antiphon sang of Stephen, who in the shower of stones found perfect joy, and, thought I, Brother Wolf has indeed found joy.

But at a later season I heard the story, when Sister Clare herself told me of his coming; how for three days with that hurt foot he lay outside their door and would not enter, though often a Sister went out to call him in. But one bitter night two Sisters talked thus: 'Nay,' said one, 'he will not come in: I must shut the door; go out again, thou, at the time of Lauds, and call once more.' And that one, being portress, promised, and the other departed, but came back. 'Sister,' she said, and I think it must have been the gentle Clare herself; 'if he comes not in at the hour of Lauds leave the door open; he will perish of cold this bitter night.' And the portress said, 'Leave the door open, Mother, in this bitter cold?' And the gentle voice said, 'It is our Little Father's Brother, my Sister; what thinkest thou?' And that Sister said, 'Ah, Mother!' and tears were in her voice. Now I am sure the wolf heard and understood, for there was a faint movement without, and when they looked, there was Wolf, rising stiffly from his doorstep where he had lain. And when they opened the door wide he crept inside, looking upon them with eyes that held them, so full of tears and pain were they. And they two, when they saw the evil case that he was in, and that foot, fell to mourning as women will, and very quickly they summoned the Sisters, though it was past Compline, and none may speak, and they had in warm water and soft oils and washed and dressed it and bound it up. And I know it was because he would not that they should be cold by reason of the door being left open that he came inside, and so love caught love, as it always will. After that he abode with them and left them no more . . .

YELLOW SPRING

Juan Ramon Jimenez

April came full
Of yellow flowers,
The brook was yellow,
The stone walls were yellow, the hill,
The children's graveyard
And the orchard where love was living.

The sun anointed the world with yellow
With down pouring rays
All through the golden lilies,
The warm golden water,
The yellow butterflies,
Over the golden roses.

Yellow garlands were climbing
Up the trees, the day
Was a grace perfumed with gold
In a golden awakening of life,
Among the bones of the dead
God opened his yellow hands.

DRAGON-FLY LOVE

William Plomer

Plated with light I float a thousand eyes,
On rustling wings of veiny talc to fly,
To kiss in flight the image of my pride
That skims the deep reflection of the sky,
Where finny shoals in shadowy grace
repose:
Insects that perish with a tiny cry
Provide the speed with which my body
goes
In scaly splendour quadruplaning by.

Giddy with hope I seize my love at noon;
On tremulous wave of fiery air we run,
Long locked in love, across the red
lagoon,
Blazing delirious while we whirl as one –
Diamonds melting underneath the
moon,
Planets in union going round the sun.

THE SNOW GOOSE

Paul Gallico

Once this lighthouse abutted on the sea and was a beacon on the Essex coast.
Time shifted land and water and its usefulness came to an end.

Lately it served again as a human habitation. In it there lived a lonely man.
His body was warped but his heart was filled with love for wild and hunted
things. He was ugly to look upon but he created great beauty... Physical
deformity often breeds hatred of humanity in men. Rhayader did not hate; he
loved very greatly, man, the animal kingdom, and all nature. His heart was
filled with pity and understanding. He had mastered his handicap, but he could
not master the rebuffs he suffered, due to his appearance. The thing that
drove him into seclusion was his failure to find anywhere a return of the
warmth that flowed from him. He repelled women. Men would have warmed
to him had they got to know him. But the mere fact that an effort was being
made hurt Rhayader and drove him to avoid the person making it ... He never
shot over a bird, and wild-fowlers were not welcome near his premises. He
was a friend to all things wild, and the wild things repaid him with this
friendship.

LITTLE THINGS

Teresa Hooley

She said, 'I cannot understand
Your passion for these little things.'
Oh, I shall never make her see
How heartbreaking and dear to me
A seagull's footprints in the sand;
A feather from a robin's wings;
The way the rose-red anthers grow
On scabious flowers, purple-blue;
The glory of a flake of snow;
The colour in a drop of dew;
Striped velvet of a bee's brown coat;

The little pinky paws of moles;
Sunlight upon a pigeon's throat;
The little lovely secret holes
Of wood-wren's nest and field-mouse run;
The curve of rose-petals; the back
Of ladybirds, bright red and black;
The silken touch of thistledown;
A fleck of seafoam in the sun;
Pebbles in pools, all wet and brown ...
Oh will she never, never see
How great these little things can be?

IN SPRINGTIME

Rudyard Kipling

My garden blazes brightly with the rose-bush and the peach,
And the koil sings above it, in the siris by the well,
From the creeper-covered trellis comes the squirrel's chattering speech,
And the blue jay screams and flutters where the cheery sat-bhai dwell.
But the rose has lost its fragrance, and the koil's note is strange;
I am sick of endless sunshine, sick of blossom-burdened bough.
Give me back the leafless woodlands where the winds of Springtime range –
Give me back one day in England, for it's Spring in England now!

Through the pines the gusts are booming, o'er the brown fields blowing chill,
From the furrow of the ploughshare steams the fragrance of the loam,
And the hawk nests on the cliffside and the jackdaw in the hill,
And my heart is back in England 'mid the sights and sounds of Home.
But the garland of the sacrifice this wealth of rose and peach is,
Oh! koil, little koil, singing on the siris bough,
In my ears the knell of exile your ceaseless bell-like speech is –
Can you tell me aught of England or of Spring in England now?

BY LOCH ETIVE

Bryan Guinness

The flowers of the flags
Are like yellow birds, hanging
Over the secret pool.

The fronds of the ferns
Are like green serpents, curling
Beside the silent path.

The lashes of your lids
Are like a bird's wing, sweeping
Across your regard.

The softness of your speech
Is like rain, falling
Among parched thoughts.

The lenience of your lips
Is like a cloud, dissolving
At the kiss of the wind.

From your deep consideration
Runs the dark stream, nourishing
The lake, the loch of my love.

THE HORSES

James Stephens

It was a delicious day. The sun was shining with all its might. One could see that it liked shining and hoped everybody enjoyed its art. If there were birds about anywhere it is certain they were singing. In this suburb, however, there were only sparrows, but they hopped and flew, and flew and hopped, and cocked their heads sideways and chirped · something cheerful, but possibly rude, as one passed. They were busy to the full extent of their beings, playing innocent games with happy little flies, and there was not one worry among a thousand of them.

There was a cat lying on a hot window ledge. She was looking drowsily at the sparrows, and anyone could see that she loved them and wished them well.

There was a dog stretched across a doorway. He was very quiet, but he was not in the least bored. He was taking a sunbath, and he was watching the cat. So steadily did he observe her that one discerned at a glance he was her friend, and would protect her at any cost.

There was a small boy who held in his left hand a tin can and a piece of string. With his right hand he was making affectionate gestures to the dog. He loved playing with animals, and he always rewarded their trust in him.

GLAD SIGHT

William Wordsworth

Glad sight wherever new with old
Is joined through some dear homeborn
    tie;
The life of all that we behold

Depends upon that mystery.
Vain is the glory of the sky,
The beauty vain of field or grove,
Unless, while with admiring eye
We gaze, we also learn to love.

THE ONCE AND FUTURE KING

T. H. White

'How does one get hold of a sword?' he continued. 'Where can I steal one? Could I waylay some knight, even if I am mounted on an ambling pad, and take his weapon by force? There must be some swordsmith or armourer in a great town like this, whose shop would be still open.'

He turned his mount and cantered off the street. There was a quiet churchyard at the end of it, with a kind of square in front of the church door. In the middle of the square there was a heavy stone with an anvil on it, and a fine new sword was stuck through the anvil.

'Well,' said the Wart, 'I suppose it is some sort of war memorial, but it will have to do. I am sure nobody would grudge Kay a war memorial, if they knew his desperate strait.'

He tied his reins round a post of the lych-gate, strode up the gravel path, and took hold of the sword.

'Come, sword,' he said. 'I must cry your mercy and take you for a better cause.'

'This is extraordinary,' said the Wart. 'I feel strange when I have hold of this sword, and I notice everything much more clearly. Look at the beautiful gargoyles of the church and of the monastery which it belongs to. See how splendidly all the famous banners in the aisle are waving. How nobly that yew holds up the red flakes of its timbers to worship God. How clean the snow is. I can smell something like feverfew and sweet briar – and is it music that I hear?'

It was music, whether of pan-pipes or of recorders, and the light in the churchyard was so clear, without being dazzling, that one could have picked a pin out twenty yards away.

'There is something in this place,' said the Wart. 'There are people. Oh, people, what do you want?'

Nobody answered him, but the music was loud and the light beautiful.

'People,' cried the Wart, 'I must take this sword. It is not for me, but for Kay. I will bring it back.'

There was still no answer, and Wart turned back to the anvil. He saw the golden letters, which he did not read, and the jewels on the pommel, flashing in the lovely light.

'Come, sword,' said the Wart.

He took hold of the handles with both hands, and strained against the stone. There was a melodious consort on the recorders, but nothing moved.

The Wart let go of the handles, when they were beginning to bite into the palms of his hands, and stepped back, seeing stars.

'It is well fixed,' he said.

He took hold of it again and pulled with all his might. The music played more strongly, and the light all about the churchyard glowed like amethysts; but the sword still stuck.

'Oh, Merlyn,' cried the Wart, 'help me to get this weapon.'

There was a kind of rushing noise, and a long chord played along with it. All round the churchyard there were hundreds of old friends. They rose over the church wall all together, like the Punch and Judy ghosts of remembered days, and there were badgers and nightingales and vulgar crows and hares and wild geese and falcons and fishes and dogs and dainty unicorns and solitary wasps and corkindrills and hedgehogs and griffins and the thousand other animals he had met. They loomed round the church wall, the lovers and helpers of the Wart, and they all spoke solemnly in turn. Some of them had come from the banners in the church, where they were painted in heraldry, some from the waters and the sky and the fields about – but all, down to the smallest shrew mouse, had come to help on account of love. Wart felt his power grow.

'Put your back into it,' said a Luce (or pike) off one of the heraldic banners, 'as you once did when I was going to snap you up. Remember that power springs from the nape of the neck.'

'What about those forearms,' asked a badger gravely, 'that are held together by a chest? Come along, my dear embryo, and find your tool.'

A Merlin sitting at the top of the yew tree cried out, 'Now then, Captain Wart, what is the first law of the foot? I thought I once heard something about never letting go?'

'Don't work like a stalling woodpecker,' urged a Tawny Owl affectionately. 'Keep up a steady effort, my duck, and you will have it yet.'

A white-front said, 'Now, Wart, if you were once able to fly the great North Sea, surely you can co-ordinate a few little wing-muscles here and there? Fold your powers together, with the spirit of your mind, and it will come out like butter. Come along, Homo sapiens, for all we humble friends of yours are waiting here to cheer.'

The Wart walked up to the great sword for the third time. He put out his right hand softly and drew it out as gently as from a scabbard.

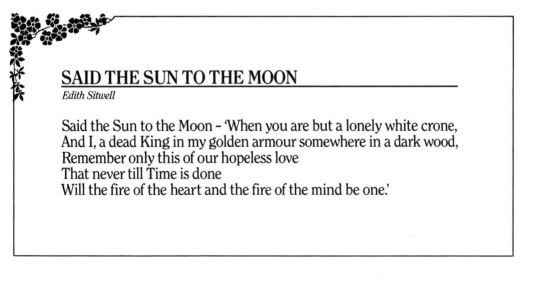

SAID THE SUN TO THE MOON

Edith Sitwell

Said the Sun to the Moon – 'When you are but a lonely white crone,
And I, a dead King in my golden armour somewhere in a dark wood,
Remember only this of our hopeless love
That never till Time is done
Will the fire of the heart and the fire of the mind be one.'

AT THE BACK OF THE NORTH WIND

George MacDonald

I know a river
whose waters run asleep
run run ever
singing in the shallows
dumb in the hollows
sleeping so deep
and all the swallows
that dip their feathers
in the hollows
or in the shallows
are the merriest swallows of all
for the nests they bake
with the clay they cake
with the water they shake
from their wings that rake
the water of the shallows
or the hollows
will hold together
in any weather and so the swallows
are the merriest fellows
and have the merriest children
and are built so narrow
like the head of an arrow
to cut the air
and go just where
the nicest water is flowing

and the nicest dust is blowing
for each so narrow
like head of an arrow
is only a barrow
to carry the mud he makes
from the nicest water flowing
and the nicest dust that is blowing
to build his nest
for her he loves best
with the nicest cakes
which the sunshine bakes
all for their merry children
all so callow
with beaks that follow
gaping and hollow
wider and wider
after their father
or after their mother
the food-provider
who brings them a spider
or a worm the poor hider
down in the earth
so there's no dearth
for their beaks as yellow
as the buttercups growing
beside the flowing
of the singing river

TO BE INTERESTED
George Santayana

To be interested in the changing seasons is a happier state of mind than to be
hopelessly in love with Spring.

THE MEANING OF FLOWERS
Claire Powell

There was a great blossoming of books on the language of flowers in early Victorian
times, almost all derived from the French master-work *Le Langage des Fleurs* by
Madame de la Tour. But the French were a little too outspoken on matters of love for
the English reader of the time, and the book was generally bowdlerised: in the
phrase of the age, 'a discretion was exercised in the rejection or alteration of those
passages not suited to the English taste'. The language of flowers was essentially a
Victorian cult, and some of the flowers that were listed are by no means common
now. But they live on in old English gardens, and it is refreshing to be reminded of the
wealth of flowers which were so well known a century ago.

Before the actual meanings attributed to the flowers could be appreciated it was
necessary to learn the code which conveyed a variation of the thought by the way in
which the flowers were presented. A flower presented in a normal upright position
was intended to convey the positive thought implicit in the 'translation' of the flower-
meaning. If the flower was given hanging down in an inverted position it conveyed
the reverse of the original thought. For example, a rosebud presented with its thorns
and leaves said plainly, 'I fear, but I hope.' Given back to the gentleman upside down,
the message was, 'You must neither fear nor hope.' There were intricate variations of
this code. If the rosebud was given stripped of its thorns, it said, 'There is everything
to hope for.' If it had been stripped of its leaves it said, 'There is everything to fear.' If
the giver intended a personal message about himself, he inclined the flower to the
left as he presented it. If he wanted to convey something about the recipient – '*You
are all purity and sweetness*,' for instance, for which the appropriate flower would be
a white lily – he would incline it to the right as he gave it; if he leant it the other way
he might be making extravagant claims about himself.

If an answer to a question was implied by the gift of a flower, to present it with the
right hand gave an affirmative and to hand it over with the left implied a negative.
When a flower was given there could be an additional message communicated by
where the recipient chose to wear it. If she put it in her hair it implied *caution*; if she
placed it in her cleavage the sign given was of *remembrance* or *friendship*; if she
placed it on her heart the clear meaning was *love*.

This cipher had its extra intricacies according to the flower. A marigold placed in
the hair meant *sorrows of the mind*; resting on the breast it announced *listlessness*
or *boredom*; over the heart it spoke of the *pangs of love*. When flowers were sent
rather than given, the maiden carefully studied the position of the knot in the ribbon
with which the bunch was tied. Looking at the bouquet from the front, if the knot
was on the left it conveyed a message about the giver; if the knot was on the right, it
made a statement, or asked a question, about the recipient.

FLORAL SYMPHONY

Pat Johnson

The rose composed a symphony -
With love poured out its heart.
The other flowers in great delight
Each clamoured for a part.

The poppy played the piccolo,
The foxglove chose the flute,
The violet, the violin.
While the lupin strummed the lute.

The daisy played the double bass,
The buttercup, bassoon.
The chrysanthemum crashed the
    cymbals!!!
And fell into a swoon ...

The sunflower almost strained itself
Playing the saxophone ...
The cornflower tried the clarinet -
But gave up with a groan.

The dahlia tried to play the drum
But went quite off its head,
So they took away the drum -
And made it play the harp instead!

The peony on piano
A virtuoso proved,
The orchid on the oboe
Left everybody moved.

The carnation as conductor
Was a most impressive sight
And rehearsed the flowers for ages
To make sure they got it right.

The symphony was a great success,
Everyone called for more.
No garden it seemed had ever been
So much in tune before!

PRAYER OF THE BADGER

George Scott Moncrieff

Lord, I do love the darkness
The hours folk call the night
Where others see but blackness
I know a lordly light.

The light that burns within
Each breathing hopeful heart
And gives all living kin
Of godliness some part.

Lord I do love the sunlight
Reflected by the moon,
I move by it at midnight
But hide from it at noon.
Your daylight dawning blinds me
Reveals me from above,
Ungainly and unkindly
Unworthy of your love.

Lord, I do love the darkness
The hours folk call the night
Where others see but starkness
I know a lordly light.

I dance between the trees
Of this cathedral wood.
I scent the gentlest breeze
And know your will is good.

NOCTURN
Francis Thompson

I walk, I only,
Not only I wake;
Nothing is, this sweet night,
But doth couch and wake
For its love's sake;
Everything, this sweet night,
Couches with its mate.
For whom but for the stealthy-visitant
   sun
Is the naked moon
Tremulous and elate?
The heaven hath the earth
Its own and all apart;
The hushed pool holdeth
A star to its heart.

You may think the rose sleepeth,
But though she folded is,
The wind doubts her sleeping;
Not all the rose sleeps,
But smiles in her sweet heart
For crafty bliss.
The wind lieth with the rose,
And when he stirs, she stirs in her
   repose:
The wind hath the rose,
And the rose her kiss.
Ah, mouth of me!
Is it then that this
Seemeth much to thee? -
I wander only.
The rose hath her kiss.

GOOD AND FAITHFUL SERVANT
W. A. Stevens

Consider the bee. He has five eyes: three simple ones on top of his head, two compound ones with thousands of lenses. And he has 5000 nostrils – nose enough to smell an apple tree two miles away. He has two sets of wings which can be hooked together in flight so they flap as one, 16,000 times a minute. And no matter how he zigzags his dizzy dance of the flowers he always bee-lines it back to his hive and his job there.

He may be a street cleaner, a water carrier, a nurse, a sentry, a mason, an engineer, or an air conditioner. If he is the last, he may fan for 12 hours at a stretch in the hive, on top of 12 hours spent gathering nectar outside. Busy as a bee is no overstatement; he literally works himself to death, all for the single teaspoon of honey spread upon your breakfast toast, the entire quota of his few short weeks of life. A one pound jar of honey represents 50,000 miles as the bee flies, or a girdling of our globe twice round.

Let us not take the bee so much for granted again. All his dipping into dandelions and daisies and snapdragons is no joyous game but an instinctive obedience to an ordinance of nature that commands 'while the earth remaineth, seedtime and harvest shall not cease.' There are 100,000 species of plants which could never properly form seeds without the bee. Without him, our bread would not be sweet: indeed there would be no bread or wine either. And so, in many churches, beeswax candles are used at the traditional service of bread-breaking and wine-drinking: it is a way of paying tribute to our good and faithful servant, the bee.

GOODBYE TO THE WEST COUNTRY

Henry Williamson

In their native soil, worms are so careful and so gentle. Under the apple trees in the garden the first flakes of blossom are lying; and, after dark, when the dew is falling, and condensing on the white petals, the worms move up their galleries from the lower earth and put out their heads and feel the night air. They listen not with ears, but with their entire bodies, which are sensitive to light and to all ground vibration. Then, feeling that it is safe, one after another begins to move out of its tunnel, and with eager pointed head, to search for petals of fallen apple-blossom. When a petal is found, it is taken in the worm's mouth and the worm withdraws into its tunnel, and leaves the petal outside the hole. Then the worm moves out again in another direction, casting about until it finds another flake. This, too, is taken to the entrance of the tunnel . . .

When the worm has, and so carefully, gathered about a dozen petals at the mouth of its tunnel, it picks them up in its mouth, one after the other, and then goes down into the darkness and eats them. Thus the night-wanderer turns blossom into the finest soil, or humus, which feeds the roots of the tree once more. Worms are soil-makers; and their galleries and tunnels act as drains to the top-soil. They are poets, choosing at their annual spring festival the choicest food and converting it, after much enjoyment, into food for the trees again. Like poets, they are the natural priests of the earth.

THE 'AH' OF WONDER

A. Samaan-Hanna

The 'Ah' of wonder
Attempting a definition,

A brief intense forgetting of self.
A leaf away from the 'me',
When the rose
Unfolds,

When the stars
Arise,

And the eyes
Widen with love
For everything that is.

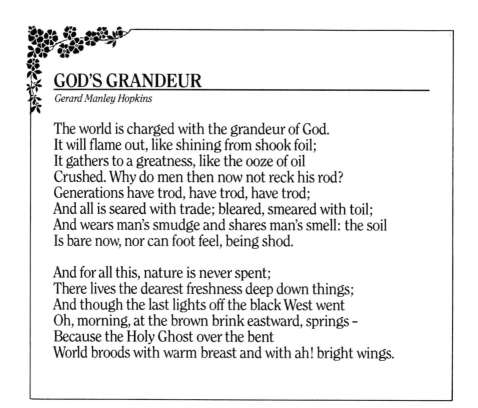

GOD'S GRANDEUR

Gerard Manley Hopkins

The world is charged with the grandeur of God.
It will flame out, like shining from shook foil;
It gathers to a greatness, like the ooze of oil
Crushed. Why do men then now not reck his rod?
Generations have trod, have trod, have trod;
And all is seared with trade; bleared, smeared with toil;
And wears man's smudge and shares man's smell: the soil
Is bare now, nor can foot feel, being shod.

And for all this, nature is never spent;
There lives the dearest freshness deep down things;
And though the last lights off the black West went
Oh, morning, at the brown brink eastward, springs –
Because the Holy Ghost over the bent
World broods with warm breast and with ah! bright wings.

THE WIND IN THE WILLOWS

Kenneth Grahame

Breathless and transfixed the Mole stopped rowing as the liquid run of that glad piping broke on him like a wave, caught him up, and possessed him utterly. He saw the tears on his comrade's cheeks, and bowed his head and understood. For a space they hung there, brushed by the purple loosestrife that fringed the bank; then the clear imperious summons that marched hand-in-hand with the intoxicating melody imposed its will on Mole, and mechanically he bent to his oars again. And the light grew steadily stronger, but no birds sang as they were wont to do at the approach of dawn; and but for the heavenly music all was marvellously still.

On either side of them, as they glided onwards, the rich meadow-grass seemed that morning of a freshness and a greenness unsurpassable. Never had they noticed the roses so vivid, the willow-herb so riotous, the meadow-sweet so odorous and pervading. Then the murmur of the approaching weir began to hold the air, and they felt a consciousness that they were nearing the end, whatever it might be, that surely awaited their expedition.

Slowly, but with no doubt or hesitation whatever, and in something of a solemn expectancy, the two animals passed through the broken, tumultuous water and moored their boat at the flowery margin of the island. In silence they landed, and pushed through the blossom and scented herbage and undergrowth that led up to the level ground, till they stood on a little lawn of a marvellous green, set round with Nature's own orchard-trees – crab-apple, wild cherry, and sloe.

'This is the place of my song-dream, the place the music played to me,' whispered the Rat, as if in a trance. 'Here, in this holy place, here if anywhere, surely we shall find Him!'

Then suddenly the Mole felt a great Awe fall upon him, an awe that turned his muscles to water, bowed his head, and rooted his feet to the ground. It was no panic terror – indeed he felt wonderfully at peace and happy – but it was an awe that smote and held him and, without seeing, he knew it could only mean that some august Presence was very, very near. With difficulty he turned to look for his friend, and saw him at his side cowed, stricken, and trembling violently. And still there was utter silence in the populous bird-haunted branches around them; and still the light grew and grew.

Perhaps he would never have dared to raise his eyes, but that, though the piping was now hushed, the call and the summons seemed still dominant and imperious. He might not refuse, were Death himself waiting to strike him instantly, once he had looked with mortal eye on things rightly kept hidden. Trembling, he obeyed, and raised his humble head; and then, in that utter clearness of the imminent dawn, while Nature, flushed with fullness of incredible colour, seemed to hold her breath for the event, he looked in the very eyes of the Friend and Helper; saw the backward sweep of the curved horns, gleaming in the growing daylight; saw the stern, hooked nose between the kindly eyes that were looking down on them humorously, while the bearded mouth broke into a half-smile at the corners; saw the rippling muscles on the arm that lay across the broad chest, the long supple hand still holding the pan-pipes only just fallen away from the parted lips; saw the splendid curves of the shaggy limbs disposed in majestic ease on the sward; saw, last of all, nestling between his very hooves, sleeping soundly in entire peace and contentment, the little, round, podgy, childish form of the baby otter. All this he saw, for one moment breathless and intense, vivid on the morning sky; and still, as he looked, he lived; and still, as he lived, he wondered.

'Rat!' he found breath to whisper, shaking. 'Are you afraid?'

'Afraid?' murmured the Rat, his eyes shining with unutterable love. 'Afraid! Of *Him*? O, never, never! And yet – and yet – O, Mole, I am afraid!'

Then the two animals, crouching to the earth, bowed their heads and did worship.

Sudden and magnificent, the sun's broad golden disc showed itself over the horizon facing them; and the first rays, shooting across the level water-meadows, took the animals full in the eyes and dazzled them. When they were able to look once more, the Vision had vanished, and the air was full of the carol of birds that hailed the dawn.

THE KING OF ELFLAND'S DAUGHTER

Lord Dunsany

When Lirazel looked upon the fields we know, as strange to her as once they had been to us, their beauty delighted her. She laughed to see the haystacks and loved their quaintness. A lark was singing and Lirazel spoke to it, and the lark seemed not to understand, but she turned to other glories of our fields, for all were new to her, and forgot the lark. It was curiously no longer the season of bluebells, for all the foxgloves were blooming and the may was gone and the wild roses were there. Alveric never understood this.

It was early morning and the sun was shining, giving soft colours to our fields, and Lirazel rejoiced in those fields of ours at more common things than one might believe there were amongst the familiar sights of Earth's every day. So glad was she, so gay with her cries of surprise and her laughter, that there seemed thenceforth to Alveric a beauty that he had never dreamed of in buttercups, and a humour in carts that he never had thought of before. Each moment she found with a cry of joyous discovery some treasure of Earth's that he had not known to be fair. And then, as he watched her bringing a beauty to our fields more delicate even than that the wild roses brought, he saw that her crown of ice had melted away.

SPELL OF CREATION

Kathleen Raine

In the flower there lies a seed,
In the seed there springs a tree,
In the tree there spreads a wood.

In the wood there burns a fire,
And in the fire there melts a stone,
Within the stone a ring of iron.

Within the ring there lies an O,
In the O there looks an eye,
In the eye there swims a sea,

And in the sea reflected sky,
And in the sky there shines the sun,
Within the sun a bird of gold.

Within the bird there beats a heart,
And from the heart there flows a song,
And in the song there sings a word.

In the word there speaks a world,
A word of joy, a world of grief,
From joy and grief there springs my
    love.

Oh love, my love, there springs a world,
And on the world there shines a sun
And in the sun there burns a fire,
In the fire consumes my heart
And in my heart there beats a bird,
And in the bird there wakes an eye,
Within the eye, earth, sea and sky,
Earth, sky and sea within an O
Lie like the seed within the flower.

LE MORTE D'ARTHUR

Sir Thomas Malory

And thus it passed on from Candlemass until after Easter that the month of May was come, when every lusty heart beginneth to blossom, and to bring forth fruit; for like as herbs and trees bring forth fruit and flourish in May, in like wise every lusty heart that is in any manner a lover, springeth and flourisheth in lusty deeds. For it giveth unto all lovers courage, that lusty month of May, in something to constrain him to some manner of thing more in that month than in any other month, for divers causes. For then all herbs and trees renew a man and woman, and likewise lovers call again to their mind old gentleness and old service, and many kind deeds that were forgotten by negligence...

    Therefore, like as May month flowereth and flourisheth in many gardens, so in like wise let every man of worship flourish his heart in this world, first unto God, and next unto the joy of them that he promised his faith unto.

THE UNICORN*

Peter Levi

There grows a living dying briar
With red rose and sharp thorn;
   Below that tree there lay a deer
With white coat and gold horn;
There was a heaven dropped a tear
The day that deer was born.
Coat of snow, unicorn,
Horn of gold, unicorn,
Heart of snow, unicorn.

There came a hunter crowned with fire
With black horse and red crown;
He blew his horn, a thing of fear,
The forest was his town.
And there beside the gentle maid
The unicorn lay down.
Coat of snow, unicorn,
Horn of gold, unicorn,
Heart of fire, unicorn.

She was as pure as any spring
With gold hair like cold fire;
And she could call and she could sing
So sweetly and so clear.
She was a heaven of singing
And to her he did draw near.
Coat of snow, unicorn,
Horn of gold, unicorn,
Heart of pain, unicorn.

They hunted him by summer light
In green dew and green fire;
The unicorn ran in their sight
The grass was young and clear.
His coat was white.
His blood was bright,
He is our hearts' desire.

Coat of snow, unicorn,
Horn of gold, unicorn,
Heart of gold, unicorn.

*The unicorn was a medieval symbol of Christ.

CARING FOR ANIMALS

Jon Silkin

I ask sometimes why these small animals
With bitter eyes, why we should care for them.

I question the sky, the serene blue water,
But it cannot say. It gives no answer.

And no answer releases in my head
A procession of grey shades patched and whimpering.

Dogs with clipped ears, wheezing cart horses
A fly without shadow and without thought.

Is it with these menaces to our vision
With this procession led by a man carrying wood

We must be concerned? The holy land, the rearing
Green island should be kindlier than this.

Yet the animals, our ghosts, need tending to.
Take in the whipped cat and the blinded owl;

Take up the man-trapped squirrel upon your shoulder.
Attend to the unnecessary beasts.

From growing mercy and a moderate love
Great love for the human animal occurs.

And your love grows. Your great love grows and grows.

THE BROTHERS KARAMAZOV

F. M. Dostoevsky

Love man even in his sin, for that already bears the semblance of divine love and is the highest love on earth. Love all God's creation, the whole of it and every grain of sand. Love every leaf, every ray of God's light! Love the animals, love the plants, love everything. If you love everything, you will perceive the divine mystery in things. And once you have perceived it, you will begin to comprehend it ceaselessly more and more every day. And you will at last come to love the whole world with an abiding, universal love. Love the animals: God has given them the rudiments of thought and untroubled joy. Do not, therefore, trouble it, do not torture them, do not deprive them of their joy, do not go against God's intent. Man, do not exalt yourself above the animals: they are without sin, while you with your majesty defile the earth by your appearance on it and you leave the traces of your defilement behind you – alas, this is true of almost every one of us! Love children especially, for they, too, like the angels, are without sin, and live to arouse tender feelings in us and to purify our hands, and are as a sort of guidance to us.

SEA FEVER

John Masefield

I must go down to the seas again, to the
  lonely sea and the sky,
And all I ask is a tall ship and a star to
  steer her by;
And the wheel's kick and the wind's song
  and the white sail's shaking,
And a grey mist on the sea's face, and a
  grey dawn breaking.

I must go down to the seas again, for the
  call of the running tide
Is a wild call and a clear call that may
  not be denied;
And all I ask is a windy day with the
  white clouds flying,
And the flung spray and the blown
  spume, and the sea-gulls crying.

I must go down to the seas again, to the
  vagrant gypsy life,
To the gull's way and the whale's way
  where the wind's like a whetted knife;
And all I ask is a merry yarn from a
  laughing fellow-rover,
And quiet sleep and a sweet dream when
  the long trick's over.

THE JOY OF WORK

Rabindranath Tagore

O giver of yourself! At the vision of you as
joy let our souls flame up to you as fire,
flow on to you as the river, permeate your
being as the fragrance of the flowers.
Give us strength to love, to love fully, our
life in its joys and sorrows, in its gains and
losses, in its rise and fall. Let us have
strength enough fully to see and hear
your universe and to work with full vigour
in it. Let us fully live the life you have
given us, let us bravely take and bravely
give. This is our prayer to you. Let us once
for all dislodge from our minds the feeble
fancy that would make out your joy to be
a thing apart from action, thin, formless,
unsustained. Wherever the peasant tills
the earth, there does joy gush out in the
green of the corn, wherever man
displaces the entangled forest, smooths
the stony ground, and clears for himself a
homestead, there does the joy enfold it in
orderliness and peace.

THE GARDEN SONG

Mallett

Plant your rows straight and long,
Temper them with prayer and song,
Mother Earth will make you strong,
If you give her love and care.

FROM THE TOMBSTONE OF A CAT, MEAFORD HALL, NEAR STONE, STAFFORDSHIRE

Earl St Vincent

'Tis false that all of Pussy's Race
Regard not person, but the Place,
For here lies one, who, could She tell
Her stories by some magic spell,
Would from the quitted barn and grove,
Her sporting haunts, to show her love
At sound of footsteps absent long
Of those she soothed with purring song,
Leap to their arms in fond embrace,
For love of them, and not for Place!

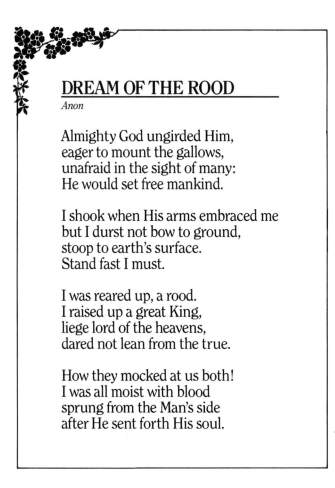

DREAM OF THE ROOD

Anon

Almighty God ungirded Him,
eager to mount the gallows,
unafraid in the sight of many:
He would set free mankind.

I shook when His arms embraced me
but I durst not bow to ground,
stoop to earth's surface.
Stand fast I must.

I was reared up, a rood.
I raised up a great King,
liege lord of the heavens,
dared not lean from the true.

How they mocked at us both!
I was all moist with blood
sprung from the Man's side
after He sent forth His soul.

Love
and
Laughter

Love and Laughter

As the saying goes, love makes the world go round, but according to Hugo Rahner, 'Without the divine drop of oil we call humour the great world machine would soon grind to a standstill.'

Laughter is medicinal. We all know there's nothing quite like 'a good laugh'. And it's my own experience that a sense of humour, which has been defined as the ability to laugh at oneself, has often been the means of keeping love on an even keel. Many a time a potentially explosive unloving situation has been defused, rescued by the release of laughter. Like love, laughter differentiates man from the beasts. The genuine laugh or its close relative, the ready smile, are signals that a person understands or at least accepts the situation, is at peace with himself. A mere warm smile often signifies affection between people.

Laughter not only releases tension but can also be an outward expression of that inner joy that the security of loving and being loved creates. During my twelve years in a monastery we followed rules of silence, but each day at a fixed hour members of the community were obliged to mix with one another and converse. This period of relaxation was called 'recreation' and I still have memories of it as being a time when the room was alive with the hum of voices punctuated by much laughter, a mixture of the gentle and the boisterous. In such situations otherwise ordinary happenings can assume humorous proportions.

Because of his capacity to think I believe man had to be endowed with the gift of laughter, so that the incongruities of life might not overwhelm him. Laughter assists man to rise above his situation just as love does. 'Seriousness,' wrote George Bernard Shaw, 'is a small man's affectation of greatness,' but laughter quickly pricks the bubble of affectation.

THE BALLAD OF THE OYSTERMAN

Oliver Wendell Holmes

It was a tall young oysterman lived by
  the river-side,
His shop was just upon the bank, his
  boat was on the tide;
The daughter of a fisherman, that was
  so straight and slim,
Lived over on the other bank, right
  opposite to him.

It was the pensive oysterman that saw
  a lovely maid,
Upon a moonlight evening, a sitting in
  the shade;
He saw her wave her handkerchief, as
  much as if to say,
'I'm wide awake, young oysterman,
  and all the folks away'.

Then up arose the oysterman, and to
  himself said he,
'I guess I'll leave the skiff at home, for
  fear that folks should see;
I read it in the story-book, that, for to
  kiss his dear,
Leander swam the Hellespont – and I
  will swim this here.'

And he has leaped into the waves,
  and crossed the shining stream,
And he has clambered up the bank,
  all in the moonlight gleam;

O there were kisses sweet as dew, and
  words as soft as rain –
But they have heard her father's step,
  and in he leaps again!

Out spoke the ancient fisherman –
  'O what was that my daughter?'
'Twas nothing but a pebble, sir, I
  threw into the water.'
'And what is that, pray tell me, love,
  that paddles off so fast?'
'It's nothing but a porpoise, sir, that's
  been a swimming past.'

Out spoke the ancient fisherman –
  'Now bring me my harpoon!
I'll get into my fishing-boat, and fix the
  fellow soon.'
Down fell that pretty innocent, as falls
  a snow-white lamb,
Her hair dropped round her pallid
  cheeks, like seaweed on a clam.

Alas for those two loving ones! she
  waked not from her swound,
And he was taken with cramp, and
  in the waves was drowned;
But Fate has metamorphosed them,
  in pity of their woe,
And now they keep an oyster-shop
  for mermaids down below.

A RHINOCEROS, SOME LADIES AND A HORSE

James Stephens

One day a great lady of the halls came in, and was received on the knee. She was very great. Her name was Maudie Darling, or thereabouts. My bosses called her nothing but 'Darling', and she called them the same. When the time came for her to arrive the whole building got palpitations of the heart. After waiting a while my thin boss got angry, and said – 'Who does the woman think she is? If she isn't here in two twos I'll go down to the entry, and when she does come I'll boot her out.' The fat boss said – 'She's only two hours late, she'll be here before the week's out.'

Within a few minutes there came great clamours from the courtyard. Patriotic cheers, such as Parnell himself never got, were thundering. My bosses ran instantly to the inner office. Then the door opened, and the lady appeared.

She was very wide, and deep, and magnificent. She was dressed in camels and zebras and goats: she had two peacocks in her hat and a rabbit muff in her hand, and she strode among these with prancings.

But when she got right into the room and saw herself being looked at by three men and a boy she became adorably shy: one could see that she had never been looked at before.

'O,' said she, with a smile that made three and a half hearts beat like one, 'O,' said she, very modestly, 'is Mr Which-of-'em-is-it really in? Please tell him that Little-Miss-Me would be so glad to see and to be –'

Then the inner door opened and the large lady was surrounded by my fat boss and my thin boss. She crooned to them – 'O, you dear boys, you'll never know how much I've thought of you and longed to see you.'

After a while they all came out again. The lady was helpless with laughter: she had to be supported by my two bosses – 'O,' she cried, 'you boys will kill me.' And the bosses laughed and laughed, and the fat one said – 'Darling, you're a scream,' and the thin one said – 'Darling, you're a riot.'

And then . . . she saw me! I saw her seeing me the very way I had seen the rhinoceros seeing me: I wondered for an instant would she smell me down one leg and up the other. She swept my two bosses right away from her, and she became a kind of queen, very glorious to behold: but sad, startled. She stretched a long, slow arm out and out and then she unfolded a long, slow finger, and pointed it at me – 'Who is THAT??' she whispered in a strange whisper that could be heard two miles off.

My fat boss was an awful liar – 'The cat brought that in,' said he.

But the thin boss rebuked him: 'No,' he said, 'it was not the cat. Let me introduce you; darling, this is James. James, this is the darling of the gods.'

'And of the pit,' said she, sternly.

She looked at me again. Then she sank to her knees and spread out both arms to me –

'Come to my boozalum, angel,' said she in a tender kind of way.

I knew what she meant, and I knew that she didn't know how to pronounce that word. I took a rapid glance at the area indicated. The lady had a boozalum you could graze a cow on. I didn't wait one second, but slid, in one swift, silent slide, under the table.

A MUTUAL PAIR

C. Brahms and S. J. Simon

'I feel certain,' said Aunt Lobelia, 'that the hussy has a past.'

'Certain to,' said Mrs Creamery darkly.

'Then why are we losing time?' demanded Aunt Lobelia. 'Set to work at once to find out what, when and where, and we will reveal it to Pelham.'

'In all its perfidy,' agreed Mrs Creamery.

But in spite of Mrs Creamery's artless cross-examination, Pumbleberry's outside enquiries, and the little servant girl's minute searching of such drawers as she could find unlocked, no guilty secret came to light. If la Cabuchon had a past they could not find it. And here she is, composed and attentive, waiting for Pelham to propose to her.

In spite of her composure she is feeling a little restless. Pelham has been babbling for three-quarters of an hour and has still only got himself as far as the high regard in which he holds her.

Patience!

Pelham is babbling on. 'You have been more than a mother to my daughters. You have been more than a friend to my mother. Will you...' he stops. His courage fails him. 'Will you,' he says, 'read to me...?'

But la Cabuchon has a headache.

Pelham is worried. 'Am I keeping you up, m'dear? Would you not like to rest upstairs?'

But la Cabuchon responds with a faint smile. No, she is not tired. It is only ... but no matter!

But Pelham is a man of the world, and it is this that gives him the right to ask for her confidence. All his experience, all his mature judgement, and such wisdom as he may possess are hers for the asking. Let her not hesitate to avail herself of them.

La Cabuchon does not hesitate. She asks.

'Mr Clutterwick,' she says, 'you have a sister–'

'Eleven,' says Pelham indulgently.

'Let us say, then, that one of them is a sister who is very foolish,' says la Cabuchon. 'And this sister is so foolish that she falls in love above her station...'

'No station is above a Clutterwick,' says Pelham reprovingly.

Farewell subtlety! Under her breath la Cabuchon curses freely. This man is so English that he cannot see his way through the broadest *blague*.

'It is not your sister,' she says. 'It is me.'

Pelham gasps. 'You!'

La Cabuchon casts her eyes down and assumes the expression of one who is blushing.

Pelham is worried. 'You are in love?'

'But yes,' says la Cabuchon.

'Very much in love?' pursues Pelham.

'But very much.'

Pelham draws a resigned breath.

'This man,' he asks, 'I hope he is worthy of you.'

'I ask myself only, am I worthy of him?' sighs la Cabuchon.

'This woman is feckless,' thinks Pelham.

'He is so kind,' continues la Cabuchon, 'so noble, so generous...'

'Yes, yes.' Pelham waves away these priggish virtues. 'But is he a man of substance? Can he provide you with the sort of life with which,' he pauses, 'you ought to be accustomed?'

'But yes,' says la Cabuchon.

Pelham is puzzled. This man, confound him, is noble, generous and wealthy. What then is worrying his darling? An awful thought strikes him. The scoundrel must be married already. But how to put such a question delicately? Tcha! This was no time for reticence.

'I think I can see your problem,' he begins. 'This man, who has been pursuing you with his intentions, is not – ahem! – free to marry.'

'Oh!' breathes la Cabuchon. 'But you are wrong, Mr Clutterwick. It is not that at all.'

Pelham is baffled.

'This man,' he gropes, 'he is perhaps too young?'

'He is just the right age.'

'Perhaps an invalid.'

'He gets very tired in the City,' says la Cabuchon, 'but nothing more.'

'Ah, yes,' says Pelham heavily, forgetting his hatred for a moment. Almost this man might have been himself. But soon his hatred flares out afresh.

Pelham decides to ask a blunt question.

'You will forgive my abruptness,' he says, 'but if this man you love is a man of substance, kind, generous, free, and,' he gulps, 'good-looking – what then is your problem?'

La Cabuchon picks up a lace handkerchief. She cannot meet his eye.

'He does not love me,' she confides.

Pelham is galvanised. He leaps to his feet.

'Not love you!' he cries. 'Impossible. Why all the world loves you. Are you not the most gracious, the most beautiful, the most...' words fail him.

But he finds that he is kneeling beside her. He finds his finger resting on his third waistcoat button. He finds himself saying: 'Forget this ingrate – let me take care of you.' He finds himself kissing her little hand.

'Ca-y-est,' thinks la Cabuchon exultantly.

SONG FOR SPRINGTIME

D. C. Yarrow

O, there is lyric laughter
In everything today,
The old leaves falling faster
'Fore the wind's artillery.
The sou'west wind a blowing,
And gushing streams a flowing.
O, there is lyric laughter
In everything today.

O, there is lyric laughter
In everything today,
The March hares getting dafter
For now there's greenery.
The merry birds a singing
And daffodillies ringing.
O, there is lyric laughter
In everything today.

Old Sandy Dhu the packman
Is wishing he was young,
For busy now is Hymen –
The marriage garland's hung.
The lance-like lightning lapwing
Is cutting sharp the blue,
And bees are getting ready
To make honey for you.

Upon the mystic ocean
There's lyric laughter too.
For everything's in motion
And merry are the crew.
The bellowed sails are flying
And spume-smoked gulls are crying.
O, there is lyric laughter
In everything today.

'AND WERE YOU PLEASED?'

Lord Dunsany

'And were you pleased?' they asked of Helen in Hell.
'Pleased?' answered she, 'when all Troy's towers fell;
And dead were Priam's sons, and lost his throne?
And such a war was fought as none had known;
And even the gods took part; and all because
Of me alone! Pleased?
I should say I was!'

MISTER PYE

Mervyn Peake

Directly Mr Pye stepped ashore he heard her voice. 'The name is Dredger,' it said.

Mr Pye lifted his head again, his thorn-shaped nose veering towards her and the rest of his round face following it, as a ship must follow its bowsprit. His little mouth continued to smile gently but it gave nothing away.

As he remained silent, Miss Dredger raised her voice as though to establish the fact of her forthright nature from the outset. 'Mr Pye, I imagine!'

Her new acquaintance removed his glasses, wiped them carefully, and re-set them on his nose.

'Who else?' he murmured. 'Who else, dear lady?'

As Miss Dredger could not think who else could possibly be Mr Pye, and had no wish to follow so foolish a train of conjecture, she blew some smoke out of her nostrils.

Mr Pye watched the smoke-jets with interest, and then, as though he were suggesting an alternative attitude to life, he drew a little box from his waistcoat pocket and helped himself to a fruit-drop.

At this, Miss Dredger raised one of her black eyebrows, and as she did so she caught sight of young Pépé – and seeing him reminded her of Mr Pye's luggage. She turned to Mr Pye, her scrubbed hands on her tweed hips.

'What have you brought with you?' she said. Mr Pye turned his gaze upon her. 'Love,' he said. 'Just . . . Love . . .' and then he transferred the fruit-drop from one cheek to the other with a flick of his experienced tongue. His fat little hands that held the lapels of his coat were quite green with the light reflected from the harbour water.

Miss Dredger's face had turned the most dreadful colour and she had shut her eyes. The smoke drifted out of her nostrils with no enthusiasm. There were some things that simply are not mentioned – unless one wishes to be offensive and embarrassing. Religion, Art, and now this new horror – Love. What on earth did the man mean?

When she opened her eyes and found herself gazing into a face so brimming with dispassionate affection she found that her anger ebbed out of her.

'What *else*?' she muttered. 'Have you brought anything *else*?'

All at once Mr Pye was as alert as a bird.

'Two suitcases and a haversack.'

WISDOM

Alice (aged 4)

You have to love your baby brother
otherwise he gets wind.

KING HENRY
Sidney (aged 7)

King Henry the eight fell in love lots of times and in the end they had to chop his head off because he was getting fat.

THE WONDERFUL O
James Thurber

Working with valour and love and hope, the islanders put the O back in everything that had lost it. The name of Goldilocks regained its laughter, and there were locks for keys, and shoes were no longer shes. A certain couple once more played their fond duets on mandolin and glockenspiel. Ophelia Oliver, who had vanished from the haunts of men, returned, wearing both her O's again. Otto Ott could say his name without a stammer, and dignity returned to human speech and English grammar. Once more a man could say boo to a goose, and tell the difference between to lose and too loose. Every family had again a roof and floor, and the head of the house could say in English, as before: 'Someone open (or close) the door.' Towers rose up again and fountains sparkled. In the spring the robin and the oriole returned. The crows were loud in caucus, and the whippoorwill sang once again at night. The wounds that Black and Littlejack had made were healed by morning-glories, columbine, and clover, and a spreading comforter of crocuses. One April morning, Andreus and Andrea were wed.

'It could have been worse,' the old man said, riding back home from the wedding. 'They might have taken A. Then we would have had no marriage, or even carriage, or any walks to walk on.' He wiped a tear from his eye. He was worrying about the loss of I, if I had been forbidden, when he came upon the lovers in a garden. 'What would have happened,' he asked them both, 'without indivisibility?'

'Or, for the matter of that,' said Andreus, 'invincible?'

'Invincible', the old man said, 'is a matter of O.'

'What O?' asked Andreus and Andrea together.

'The O, lest we forget,' the old man said, 'in freedom.'

Suddenly their thoughtful silence was changed to laughter. 'Squck his thrug,' they heard the parrot squawking.

'He must have missed the ship,' said Andrea.

'And now he has the freedom of screech,' said Andreus.

THE NAPOLEON OF NOTTING HILL

G. K. Chesterton

'You and I, Auberon Quin, have both of us throughout our lives been again and again called mad. And we are mad. We are mad, because we are not two men but one man. We are mad, because we are two lobes of the same brain, and that brain has been cloven in two. And if you ask for the proof of it, it is not hard to find. It is not merely that you, the humourist, have been in these dark days stripped of the joy of gravity. It is not merely that I, the fanatic, have had to grope without humour. It is that though we seem to be opposite in everything, we have been opposite like man and woman, aiming at the same moment at the same practical thing. We are the father and the mother of the Charter of the Cities.'

Quin looked down at the *débris* of leaves and timber, the relics of the battle and stampede, now glistening in the glowing daylight, and finally said –

'Yet nothing can alter the antagonism – the fact that I laughed at these things and you adored them.'

Wayne's wild face flamed with something god-like as he turned it to be struck by the sunrise.

'I know of something that will alter that antagonism, something that is outside us, something that you and I have all our lives perhaps taken too little account of. The equal and eternal human being will alter that antagonism, for the human being sees no real antagonism between laughter and respect, the human being, the common man, whom mere geniuses like you and me can only worship like a god. When dark and dreary days come, you and I are necessary, the pure fanatic, the pure satirist. We have between us remedied a great wrong. We have lifted the modern cities into that poetry which every one who knows mankind knows to be immeasurably more common than the commonplace. But in healthy people there is no war between us. We are but the two lobes of the brain of a ploughman. Laughter and love are everywhere. The cathedrals, built in the ages that loved God, are full of blasphemous grotesques. The mother laughs continually at the child, the lover laughs continually at the lover, the wife at the husband, the friend at the friend. Auberon Quin, we have been too long separated, let us go out together. You have a halberd and I a sword, let us start our wanderings over the world. For we are its two essentials. Come, it is already day.'

In the blank white light Auberon hesitated a moment. Then he made the formal salute with his halberd, and they went away together into the unknown world.

MARRIAGE MARKET

Anon

These panting damsels, dancing for their
    lives,
Are only maidens waltzing into wives.
Those smiling matrons are appraisers
    sly,
Who regulate the dance, the squeeze,
    the sigh,
And each base cheapening buyer having
    chid,
Knock down their daughters to the
    noblest bid!

PIOUS SELINDA

William Congreve

Pious Selinda goes to prayers,
    If I but ask the favour;
And yet the tender fool's in tears,
    When she believes I'll leave her.

Would I were free from this restraint,
    Or else had hopes to win her!
Would she could make of me a saint,
    Or I of her a sinner!

JOHN AND MARY

Anon

John and Mary had been walking out
together for a quarter of a century. Finally
Mary plucked up her courage and said to
John, 'We've been going out together for
so long, John, that everyone in this village is talking.'
    John said, 'What are they saying,
Mary?'
    'They're saying we should get mar-
ried, John,' she answered.
    John shook his head slowly, 'Ah shure,
Mary, who'd have us!'

SONG TO BE SUNG BY THE FATHER OF INFANT FEMALE CHILDREN

Ogden Nash

My heart leaps up when I behold
A rainbow in the sky;
Contrariwise, my blood runs cold
When little boys go by.
For little boys as little boys,
No special hate I carry,
But now and then they grow to men,
And when they do, they marry.
No matter how they tarry,
Eventually they marry.
And, swine among the pearls,
They marry little girls.

Oh, somewhere, somewhere, an infant
    plays,
With parents who feed and clothe him.
Their lips are sticky with pride and
    praise,
But I have begun to loathe him.
Yes, I loathe with a loathing shameless
This child who to me is nameless.
This bachelor child in his carriage
Gives never a thought to marriage,
But a person can hardly say knife
Before he will hunt him a wife.

I never see an infant (male),
A-sleeping in the sun,
Without I turn a trifle pale
And think, is *he* the one?

Oh, first he'll want to crop his curls,
And then he'll want a pony,
And then he'll think of pretty girls
And holy matrimony.
He'll put away his pony,
And sigh for matrimony.
A cat without a mouse
Is he without a spouse.

Oh, somewhere he bubbles bubbles of
   milk,
And quietly sucks his thumbs;
His cheeks are roses painted on silk,
And his teeth are tucked in his gums.
But alas, the teeth will begin to grow,
And the bubbles will cease to bubble;
Given a score of years or so,
The roses will turn to stubble.
He'll send a bond, or he'll write a book,
And his eyes will get that acquisitive
   look,
And raging and ravenous for the kill,
He'll boldly ask for the hand of Jill.
This infant whose middle
Is diapered still
Will want to marry
My daughter Jill.

Oh sweet be his slumber and moist his
   middle!
My dreams, I fear, are infanticiddle.
A fig for embryo Lohengrins!
I'll open all of his safety pins,
I'll pepper his powder and salt his bottle,
And give him readings from Aristotle,
Sand for his spinach I'll gladly bring,
And tabasco sauce for his teething ring,
And an elegant, elegant alligator
To play with in his perambulator.
Then perhaps he'll struggle through fire
   and water
To marry somebody else's daughter!

QUEER PEOPLE

Charles G. Leland

Now a gradual sensation emotioned this
    our Gale,
That he'd seldom seen so fine a man for
    cheek as Mr. Dale;
Yet simultaneous he felt that he was all
    the while
The biggest dude and cock-a-hoop
    within a hundred mile.

For the usual expression of his quite
    enormous eyes
Was that of two ripe gooseberries
    who've been decreed a prize;
Like a goose apart from berries, too -
    though not removed from sauce -
He conversed on lovely Woman as if he
    were all her boss.

Till, in fact, he stated plainly that,
    between his face and cash,
There was not a lady living whom he was
    not sure to mash;
The wealthiest, the loveliest, of families
    sublime,
At just a single look from him must all
    give in in time.

Now when our Dale had got along so far
    upon this strain,
They saw a Dream of Loveliness
    descending from the train,
A proud and queenly beauty of a
    transcendental face,
With gloves unto her shoulders, and the
    most expensive lace.

All Baltimore and New Orleans seemed
    centred into one,
As if their stars of beauty had been fused
    into a sun;
But, oh! her frosty dignity expressed a
    kind of glow
Like sunshine when thermometers show
    thirty grades below.

But it flashed a gleam of shrewdness
    into the head of Gale,
And with aggravatin' humour he
    exclaimed to Mr.Dale,
'Since every girl's a cricket-ball and
    you're the only bat,
If you want to show you're champion, go
    in and mash on that.

'I will bet a thousand dollars, and plank
    them on the rub,
That if you try it thither, you will catch a
    lofty snub.
I don't mean but what a lady may reply
    to what you say,
But I bet you cannot win her into
    wedding in a day.'

A singular emotion enveloped Mr.Dale;
One would say he seemed confuseled,
    for his countenance was pale:
At first there came an angry look, and
    when that look did get,
He larft a wild and hollow larf, and said,
    'I take the debt.'

'The brave deserve the lovely - every
  woman may be won;
What men have fixed before us may by
  other men be done.
You will lose your thousand dollars. For
  the first time in my life
I have gazed upon a woman whom I
  wish to make my wife.'

Like a terrier at a rabbit, with his hat
  upon his eyes,
Mr. Dale, the awful masher, went head-
  longing at the prize,
Looking rather like a party simply bent
  to break the peace.
Mr. Gale, with smiles, expected just a
  yell for the police.

Oh! what are women made of? Oh! what
  can women be?
From Eves to Jersey Lilies what
  bewildering sights we see!
One listened on the instant to all the
  Serpent said;
The other paid attention right away to
  Floral Ned.

With a blow as with a hammer the
  intruder broke the ice,
And the proud and queenly beauty
  seemed to think it awful nice.
Mr. Gale, as he beheld it, with a
  trembling heart began
To realize he really was a most
  astonished man.

Shall I tell you how he wooed her? Shall
  I tell you how he won?
How they had a hasty wedding ere the
  evening was done?
For when all things were considered, the
  fond couple thought it best -
Such things are not uncommon in the
  wild and rapid West.

Dale obtained the thousand dollars, and
  then vanished with the dream.
Gale stayed in town with sorrow, like a
  spoon behind the cream,
Till one morning in the paper he read,
  though not in rhymes,
How a certain blooming couple had
  been married fifty times!

How they wandered o'er the country,
  how the bridegroom used to bet
He would wed the girl that evening -
  how he always pulled the debt;
How his eyes were large and greensome;
  how, in fact, to end the tale,
Their very latest victim was a fine young
  man named Gale!

THE IMPORTANCE OF BEING EARNEST

Oscar Wilde

MERRIMAN: [*Looks at* CECILY, *who makes no sign.*] Yes, Sir. [MERRIMAN *retires.*]

CECILY: Uncle Jack would be very much annoyed if he knew you were staying on till next week, at the same hour.

ALGERNON: Oh, I don't care about Jack. I don't care for anybody in the whole world but you. I love you, Cecily. You will marry me, won't you?

CECILY: You silly boy! Why, we have been engaged for the last three months.

ALGERNON: For the last three months?

CECILY: Yes, it will be exactly three months on Thursday.

ALGERNON: But how did we become engaged?

CECILY: Well, ever since dear Uncle Jack first confessed to us that he had a younger brother who was very wicked and bad, you of course have formed the chief topic of conversation between myself and Miss Prism. And of course a man who is much talked about is always very attractive. One feels there must be something in him, after all. I daresay it was foolish of me, but I fell in love with you, Ernest.

ALGERNON: Darling. And when was the engagement actually settled?

CECILY: On the 14th of February last. Worn out by your entire ignorance of my existence, I determined to end the matter one way or the other, and after a long struggle with myself I accepted you under this dear old tree here. The next day I bought this little ring in your name, and this is the little bangle with the true lover's knot I promised you always to wear.

ALGERNON: Did I give you this? It's very pretty, isn't it?

CECILY: Yes, you've wonderfully good taste, Ernest. It's the excuse I've always given for your leading such a bad life. And this is the box in which I keep all your dear letters. [*Kneels at table, opens box, and produces letters tied up with blue ribbon.*]

ALGERNON: My letters! But, my own sweet Cecily, I have never written you any letter.

CECILY: You need hardly remind me of that, Ernest. I remember only too well that I was forced to write your letters for you. I wrote always three times a week, and sometimes oftener.

ALGERNON: Oh, do let me read them, Cecily?

CECILY: Oh, I couldn't possibly. They would make you far too conceited. [*Replaces box.*] The three you wrote me after I had broken off the engagement are so beautiful, and so badly spelled, that even now I can hardly read them without crying a little.

ALGERNON: But was our engagement ever broken off?

CECILY: Of course it was. On the 22nd of last March. You can see the entry if you like. [*Shows diary.*] 'To-day I broke off my engagement with Ernest. I feel it is better to do so. The weather still continues charming.'

ALGERNON: But why on earth did you break it off? What had I done? I had done nothing at all. Cecily, I am very much hurt indeed to hear you broke it off. Particularly when the weather was so charming.

CECILY: It would hardly have been a really serious engagement if it hadn't been broken off at least once. But I forgave you before the week was out.

ALGERNON: [*Crossing to her, and kneeling.*] What a perfect angel you are, Cecily.

CECILY: You dear romantic boy. [*He kisses her, she puts her fingers through his hair.*] I hope your hair curls naturally, does it?

ALGERNON: Yes, darling, with a little help from others.
CECILY: I am so glad.
ALGERNON: You'll never break off our engagement again, Cecily?

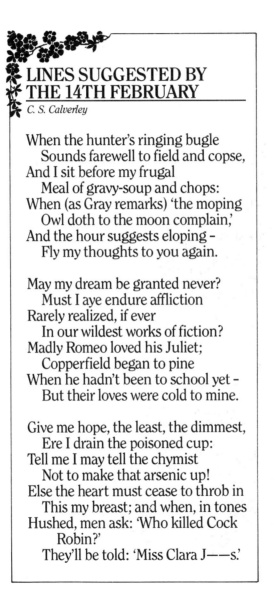

LINES SUGGESTED BY THE 14TH FEBRUARY

C. S. Calverley

When the hunter's ringing bugle
    Sounds farewell to field and copse,
And I sit before my frugal
    Meal of gravy-soup and chops:
When (as Gray remarks) 'the moping
    Owl doth to the moon complain,'
And the hour suggests eloping –
    Fly my thoughts to you again.

May my dream be granted never?
    Must I aye endure affliction
Rarely realized, if ever
    In our wildest works of fiction?
Madly Romeo loved his Juliet;
    Copperfield began to pine
When he hadn't been to school yet –
    But their loves were cold to mine.

Give me hope, the least, the dimmest,
    Ere I drain the poisoned cup:
Tell me I may tell the chymist
    Not to make that arsenic up!
Else the heart must cease to throb in
    This my breast; and when, in tones
Hushed, men ask: 'Who killed Cock
        Robin?'
    They'll be told: 'Miss Clara J——s.'

THE TERROR OF ST. TRINIANS

D. B. Wyndham Lewis and R. Searle

'Miss Languish – Chloë! Most exquisite of your sex! Believe me when I say that this – this lady's unhappy love for me is (or until I saw you, was) the greatest misery of my life. Such charm, such allure, such masterful qualities as I possess, such extreme good looks as are generally attributed to me, seemed until the moment of our meeting the most fatal of gifts. How often have I cursed them! How often have I seemed to myself fated ineluctably to fly for ever, like the shepherd Hermes, the advances of a myriad beauties for whom my frozen heart could never beat, wooed they never so cunningly! In this particular and rather pitiable case –'

He indicated Miss Fridge with a light courteous gesture.

'Don't forget the cheap engagement-ring you gave me,' snarled Miss Fridge between clenched teeth.

'I am coming to that in a moment,' said Rupert Rover. Flinging back his raven locks with an impatient gesture he continued: 'Miss Languish! I ask you most urgently to believe that my heart is henceforth irrevocably yours, whate'er betide. I may refer to this fact again and again before I have finished. I wish to impress it on you most forcibly. It is of major importance. For the single purpose of seeing you once more, my divine Chloë,' said Mr Rover with strong emotion, 'I have stooped to this ignoble masquerade and braved a myriad risks . . . I have likewise endured – what is chiefly insufferable to a proud spirit – contemptuous comments from the female proletariat on my deliberately unattractive make-up as the mythical Beaver, even to blacking out a couple of front teeth. All this deceit is justified and hallowed, Chloë, by the simple fact that I worship you devotedly and believe you to adore me, on your part, with all the ardency of a sweet and unspoiled English nature.'

Glancing at his watch, Rupert Rover resumed, more rapidly:

'The ring to which Miss Fridge has so pointedly referred was derived originally from a Christmas cracker, and placed on Miss Fridge's fourth left-hand finger by myself, in a mood of careless merriment, at an Eights Week dance two years ago . . .'

SYMPATHY

Reginald Heber

A knight and a lady once met in a grove,
While each was in quest of a fugitive
  love;
A river ran mournfully murmuring by,
And they wept in its waters for
  sympathy.

'Oh, never was knight such a sorrow
  that bore!'
'Oh, never was maid so deserted before!'
'From life and its woes let us instantly
  fly,
And jump in together for company!'

They search'd for an eddy that suited the
  deed,
But here was a bramble and there was a
  weed;
'How tiresome it is!' said the fair with a
  sigh;
So they sat down to rest them in
  company.

They gazed at each other, the maid and
  the knight;
How fair was her form, and how goodly
  his height!
'One mournful embrace,' sobb'd the
  youth, 'ere we die!'
So kissing and crying kept company.

'Oh, had I but loved such an angel as
  you!'
'Oh, had but my swain been a quarter as
  true!'
'To miss such perfection how blinded
  was I!'
Sure now they were excellent company!

At length spoke the lass, 'twixt a smile
  and a tear,
'The weather is cold for a watery bier;
When summer returns we may easily
  die -
Till then let us sorrow in company!'

MAN AT PLAY

Hugo Rahner

The 'grave-merry' man is really always two men in one: he is a man with an easy gaiety of spirit, one might almost say a man of spiritual elegance, a man who feels himself to be living in invincible security; but he is also a man of tragedy, a man of laughter and tears, a man, indeed, of gentle irony, for he sees through the tragically ridiculous masks of the game of life and has taken the measure of the cramping boundaries of our earthly existence.

And so, only one who can fuse these two contradictory elements into a spiritual unity is indeed a man who truly plays. If he is only the first of these two things, we must write him down as a frivolous person who has, precisely, played himself out. If he is only the second, then we must account him as one who cannot conquer despair. It is the synthesis of the two things that makes Homo Ludens, the 'grave-merry' man, the man with a gentle sense of humour who laughs despite his tears, and finds in all earthly mirth a sediment of insufficiency...

The man who truly plays is, therefore, first of all, a man in whom seriousness and gaiety are mingled; and, indeed, at the bottom of all play there lies a tremendous secret. All play – just as much as every task which we set ourselves to master with real earnestness of purpose – is an attempt to approximate to the Creator, who performs his work with the divine seriousness which its meaning and purpose demand, and yet with the spontaneity and effortless skill of the great artist he is, creating because he wills to create and not because he must...

This happy mingling of the light-hearted and the serious is a flower that grows only midway betwixt heaven and earth – in the *man who loves this bright and colourful world* and yet can smile at it, who knows in his heart that it has proceeded from God but also knows its limits. Within those limits, and because of them, things knock into each other, thus producing comedy – but also tragedy. These may annoy us; we can react angrily or we can accept them with calm good humour. They can disconcert us and still, at the same time, delight us in our vision directed always towards the Logos in his 'co-fashioning' action, for it is in him that everything has its source and it is towards the vision of him that all our play ultimately tends.

THERE WAS A YOUNG LADY FROM WANTAGE

Anon

There was a young lady from Wantage
Of whom the town clerk took advantage.
Said the borough surveyor:
'Indeed you must pay 'er.
You've totally altered her frontage.'

THE KISS

Coventry Patmore

'I saw you take his kiss!' ''Tis true.'
'Oh modesty!' ''Twas strictly kept:
He thought me asleep; at least, I knew
He thought I thought he thought I
   slept.'

LOVEY-DOVEY

Harold Morland

Poets call the dove
The symbol of pure love;
But have you heard the things they do?
COO!

UNDER MILK WOOD

Dylan Thomas

MR EDWARDS: Myfanwy Price!

MISS PRICE: Mr Mog Edwards!

MR EDWARDS: I am a draper mad with love. I love you more than all the flannelette and calico, candlewick, dimity, crash and merino, tussore, cretonne, crepon, muslin, poplin, ticking and twill in the whole Cloth Hall of the world. I have come to take you away to my Emporium on the hill, where the change hums on wires. Throw away your little bedsocks and your Welsh wool knitted jacket, I will warm the sheets like an electric toaster, I will lie by your side like the Sunday roast.

MISS PRICE: I will knit you a wallet of forget-me-not blue, for the money to be comfy. I will warm your heart by the fire so that you can slip it in under your vest when the shop is closed.

MR EDWARDS: Myfanwy, Myfanwy, before the mice gnaw at your bottom drawer will you say

MISS PRICE: Yes, Mog, yes, Mog, yes, yes, yes.

MR EDWARDS: And all the bells of the tills of the town shall ring for our wedding. [*Noise of money-tills and chapel bells*]

THE YOUNG VISITERS

Daisy Ashford (aged 8)

Next morning while imbibing his morning tea beneath his pink silken quilt Bernard decided he must marry Ethel with no more delay. I love the girl he said to himself and she must be mine but I somehow feel I can not propose in London it would not be seemly in the city of London. We must go for a day in the country and when surrounded by the gay twittering of the birds and the smell of the cows I will lay my suit at her feet and he waved his arm wildly at the gay thought. Then he sprang from bed and gave a rat tat at Ethel's door.

Are you up my dear he called.

Well not quite said Ethel hastilly jumping from her downy nest.

Be quick cried Bernard I have a plan to spend a day near Windsor Castle and we will take our lunch and spend a happy day.

O Hurrah shouted Ethel I shall soon be ready as I had my bath last night so wont wash very much now.

No dont said Bernard and added in a rarther fervent tone through the chink of the door you are fresher than the rose my dear no soap could make you fairer.

Then he dashed off very embarrased to dress. Ethel blushed and felt a bit excited as she heard the words and she put on a new white muslin dress in a fit of high spirits. She looked very beautifull with some red roses in her hat and the dainty red ruge in her cheeks looked quite the thing. Bernard heaved a sigh and his eyes flashed as he beheld her and Ethel thorght to herself what a fine type of manhood he reprisented with his nice thin legs in pale broun trousers and well fitting spats and a red rose in his button hole and rarther a sporting cap which gave him a great air with its quaint check and little flaps to pull down if necessary. Off they started the envy of all the waiters.

They arrived at Windsor very hot from the jorney and Bernard at once hired a boat to row his beloved up the river. Ethel could not row but she much enjoyed seeing the tough sunburnt arms of Bernard tugging at the oars as she lay among the rich cushons of the dainty boat. She had a rarther lazy nature but Bernard did not know of this. However he soon got dog tired and sugested lunch by a mossy bank.

Oh yes said Ethel quicly opening the sparkling champaigne.

Dont spill any cried Bernard as he carved some chicken.

They eat and drank deeply of the charming viands ending up with merangs and choclates.

Let us now bask under the spreading trees said Bernard in a passiunate tone.

Oh yes lets said Ethel and she opened her dainty parasole and sank down upon the long green grass. She closed her eyes but she was far from asleep. Bernard sat beside her in profound silence gazing at her pink face and long wavy eye lashes. He puffed at his pipe for some moments while the larks gaily caroled in the blue sky. Then he edged a trifle closer to Ethels form.

Ethel he murmered in a trembly voice.

Oh what is it said Ethel hastily sitting up.

Words fail me ejaculated Bernard horsly my passion for you is intense he added fervently. It has grown day and night since I first beheld you.

Oh said Ethel in supprise I am not prepared for this and she lent back against the trunk of the tree.

Bernard placed one arm tightly round her. When will you marry me Ethel he uttered you must be my wife it has come to that I love you so intensly that if you say no I shall perforce dash my body to the brink of yon muddy river he panted wildly.

O dont do that implored Ethel breathing rarther hard.

Then say you love me he cried.

Oh Bernard she sighed fervently I certinly love you madly you are to me like a heathen god she cried looking at his manly form and handsome flashing face I will indeed marry you.

THE BEST OF MYLES

Flann O'Brien

Chapman once fell in love and had not been long plying his timid attentions when it was brought to his notice that he had a rival. This rival, a ferocious and burly character, surprised Chapman in the middle of a tender conversation with the lady and immediately challenged him to a duel, being, as he said, prohibited from breaking him into pieces there and then merely by the presence of the lady.

Chapman, who was no duellist, went home and explained what had happened to Keats.

'And I think he means business,' he added. 'I fear it is a case of "pistols for two, coffee for one". Will you be my second?'

'Certainly,' Keats said, 'and since you have the choice of weapons I think you should choose swords rather than pistols.'

Chapman agreed. The rendezvous was duly made and one morning at dawn Keats and Chapman drove in a cab to the dread spot. The poet had taken the 'coffee for one' remark rather too literally and had brought along a small quantity of coffee, sugar, milk, a coffee-pot, a cup, saucer and spoon, together with a small stove and some paraffin.

After the usual formalities, Chapman and the rival fell to sword-play. The two men fought fiercely, edging hither and thither about the sward. Keats, kneeling and priming the stove, was watching anxiously and saw that his friend was weakening. Suddenly, Chapman's guard fell and his opponent drew back to plunge his weapon home. Keats, with a lightning flick of his arm took up the stove and hurled it at the blade that was poised to kill! With such force and aim so deadly was the stove hurled that it smashed the blade in three places. Chapman was saved!

The affair ended in bloodless recriminations. Chapman was warm in his thanks to Keats.

'You saved my life,' he said, 'by hurling the stove between our blades. You're tops!'

'Primus inter parries,' Keats said.

Love
and
Art

Love and Art

A successful painter friend of mine once told me that she wrote a book for publication sending up art and art connoisseurs but found that subsequently it took her a long time to get back to serious painting. Analysing it for herself afterwards she concluded that ridicule and mockery betrayed a lack of love and that love was an essential ingredient in her approach to her work.

Presuming the basic talent and a sense of beauty, painstaking care and aimed-at-perfection are vital elements in a work of art. They constitute as it were the solid surrounding structure within which the divine spark can have free play and, all being well, ignite into a God-fed, man-nourishing fire. All that special care bespeaks a certain love which is what Solzhenitsyn may have meant by the rule of the last inch:

Now listen to the rule of the last inch. The realm of the last inch. The job is almost finished, the goal almost attained, everything possible seems to have been achieved, every difficulty overcome – and yet the quality is not there ... In that moment of weariness and self-satis-faction, the temptation is greatest to give up, not to strive for the peak of quality. That's the realm of the last inch ... The rule of the last inch is simply this – not to leave it undone. And not to put it off – because otherwise your mind loses touch with that realm. And not to mind how much time you spend on it, because the aim is not to finish the job quickly but to reach perfection.

In one way or another love is bound up with what the artist does. Those who work with stone, wood or clay will tell you how they love the very touch of their media. The performing musician's communication with his audience will be commensurate with the measure of love with which he suffuses his work. It's been said that the successful painter of icons is not merely a gifted painter but a true lover of the sacred subjects he depicts and that unless he is full of this love, that special spiritual quality will be missing from the finished painting.

The task of the artist is to feed the world with beauty and as Maritain says: 'The artist is faced with an immense and desert sea and the mirror he holds up to it is no bigger than his own heart.'

BRIGHT IS THE RING OF WORDS

Robert Louis Stevenson

Bright is the ring of words
  When the right man rings them,
Fair the fall of songs
  When the singer sings them.

Still they are carolled and said –
  On wings they are carried –
After the singer is dead
  And the maker buried.

Low as the singer lies
  In the field of heather,
Songs of his fashion bring
  The swains together.

And when the west is red
  With the sunset embers,
The lover lingers and sings
  And the maid remembers.

THE LOST WORLD OF THE KALAHARI

Laurens van der Post

We found that this love of music was not peculiar to our own close group but characteristic of all these people in the desert, bearing out the tradition of the Bushman's skill as a musician and his deep devotion to music. Once, far away from our sip-wells, while resting in the middle of a hunt in the heat of a terrible day, I heard cries for help. We all sat up, alarmed, and soon there came staggering through the bush a little group of Bushmen in grave difficulties. They had seen the smoke of the fire made for our noonday tea and come straight to it. They had had no water for many days and were weak and hungry, their eyes bright with a light I had last seen on the faces of my starving fellow prisoners in a Japanese prison of war camp. As they sat down in our shade a woman started scraping with a bone at the one desert bulb left, catching the scrapings in her hand and wringing some thick white drops from it straight into the mouth of a child with black, cracked lips. I tried it and it tasted like gall. They were still a day's march from permanent water and though Ben and Dabe said they could have made it on their own, I doubted it. But the moment they had drunk from our water they produced a lyre and began to make music.

'What is the music saying, Dabe?' I asked.

'It says, "thank you", Master,' he answered with a rare smile, waving his hands towards the sky and burning desert around us.

We concluded music was as vital as water, food, and fire to them for we never found a group so poor or desperate that they did not have some musical instrument with them.

CREATIVE INTUITION IN ART AND POETRY
Jacques Maritain

We see that the fine arts, though they are more fully intellectual than the useful arts, imply, however, a much greater and more essential part played by the appetite, and require that the love for beauty should make the intellect co-natured with beauty. Because, in the last analysis, in art as in contemplation, intellectuality at its peak goes beyond concepts and discursive reason, and is achieved through a congeniality or con-naturality with the object, which love alone can bring about. To produce in beauty the artist must be in love with beauty. Such undeviating love is a supra-artistic rule – a precondition, not sufficient as to the ways of making, yet necessary as to the vital animation of art – which is presupposed by all the rules of art.

MAN AT PLAY
Hugo Rahner

The harmony between the artist's body and soul which is the ultimate mystery of the dance is, however, but part of a larger whole, for in the dance there is also a cosmic mystery. It is an attempt to move in time with that creative love that 'made the sun and the other stars'. It is once again Lucian, that 'serious-merry' man, who writes: 'Those who most accurately describe the genealogy of the dancer's art, declare that its origin is the same as that of the world itself, and that it appeared together with that primal eros that is the beginning of all things; for what is that dance of the stars, what is that regular intertwining of the planets with the fixed stars, what are the common measure and sweet harmonies of their movements – what are all these things but repetitions of that great dance that was in the beginning?'

THE LORD OF THE DANCE
Anthony Duncan

The whole creation is dancing; the whole universe – galaxies, nebulae, stars and their satellites – is engaged in the Great Dance. They turn, and come together, and draw apart, and come together again. And so it has ever been, and so it shall ever be through all eternity.

Creation makes it own music. There is no created being that does not sing, and the music of everything that is joins together to make the great Harmony and Rhythm of the Dance. Everything that exists treads the same measure, each according to its own rhythm, and every individual rhythm is related to, and is an integral part of, the Rhythm of the Dance. These rhythms are reflected in the life-cycle of beings, and there is no part of creation which does not have its own life-cycle, whether they be creatures of a day, like some insects, or plants, or trees, or men, the rocks and the rivers, and earth itself, the stars and indeed the whole universe as it is known to man ... The whole Universe is a dance measure, and the measure of the Dance itself determines the shapes and patterns of creation. The Measure, and the Rhythm of the Measure are one and the same, and everything that exists expresses the central theme of the Dance, each in its own way. This central theme is Love.

MUSIC
Walter de la Mare

When music sounds, gone is the earth I know,
And all her lovely things even lovelier grow;
Her flowers in vision flame, her forest trees
Lift burdened branches, stilled with ecstasies.

When music sounds, out of the water rise
Naiads whose beauty dims my waking eyes,
Rapt in strange dreams burns each enchanted face,
With solemn echoing stirs their dwelling-place.

When music sounds, all that I was I am
Ere to this haunt of brooding dust I came;
And from Time's woods break into distant song
The swift-winged hours, as I hasten along.

THE FELLOWSHIP OF THE RING
J. R. R. Tolkien

The Elves next unwrapped and gave to each of the Company the clothes they had brought. For each they had provided a hood and cloak, made according to his size, of the light but warm silken stuff that the Galadhrim wove. It was hard to say of what colour they were: grey with the hue of twilight under the trees they seemed to be; and yet if they were moved, or set in another light, they were green as shadowed leaves, or brown as fallow fields by night, dusk-silver as water under the stars. Each cloak was fastened about the neck with a brooch like a green leaf veined with silver.
  'Are these magic cloaks?' asked Pippin, looking at them with wonder.
  'I do not know what you mean by that,' answered the leader of the Elves. 'They are fair garments, and the web is good, for it was made in this land. They are elvish robes certainly, if that is what you mean. Leaf and branch, water and stone: they have the hue and beauty of all these things under the twilight of Lórien that we love; for we put the thought of all that we love into all that we make. Yet they are garments, not armour, and they will not turn shaft or blade. But they should serve you well: they are light to wear, and warm enough or cool enough at need. And you will find them a great aid in keeping out of the sight of unfriendly eyes, whether you walk among the stones or the trees. You are indeed high in the favour of the Lady! For she herself and her maidens wove this stuff; and never before have we clad strangers in the garb of our own people.'

IN GOD'S UNDERGROUND

Richard Wurmbrand

We were very quiet when he ceased singing. The guards, huddled in their quarters around a coke stove, did not stir all evening. We began to tell stories, and when I was asked for one, I thought of the song, and told them this old Jewish legend:

King Saul of Israel brought David, the shepherd honoured for killing Goliath, to his court. David loved music, and he was delighted to see a harp of great beauty standing in the palace. Saul said, 'I paid much for that instrument, but I was deceived. It gives forth only ugly sounds.'

David took it up to try, and drew from it music so exquisite that every man was moved. The harp seemed to laugh and sing and weep. King Saul asked, 'How is it that all the musicians I called brought discord from this harp, and only you could bring out music?'

David, the future king, replied, 'Before me, each man tried to play his own song on these strings. But I sang to the harp its own song. I recalled how it had been a young tree, with birds that chirped in its branches and limbs green with leaves that blossomed in the sun. I reminded it of the day when men came to cut it down; and you heard it weep under my fingers. I explained then that this is not the end. Its death as a tree meant the start of a new life in which it would glorify God, as a harp; and you heard how it rejoiced under my hands.

'So when the Messiah comes, many will try to sing on his harp their own songs, and their tunes will be harsh. We must sing on His harp His own song, the song of His life, passions, joys, sufferings, death and resurrection. Only then will the music be true.' It was a song like this we heard that Christmas in the jail of Tirgul-Ocna.

MARIA: BEYOND THE CALLAS LEGEND

Arianna Stassinopoulos

If what art brings to us is in itself only one half of the experience, the other half being what we bring to art, then part of Maria [Callas's] greatness was to *make* the audience bring more to the experience, and give more of themselves to it. She did this as well as bringing more of herself to the part [of Tosca] than anyone else before her ... 'What will-power must have gone into your career,' an interviewer exclaimed once. Maria corrected him: 'Not will-power. Love...'

THOU TAKEST THE PEN

Dag Hammarskjold

Thou takest the pen – and the lines dance.
Thou takest the flute – and the notes shimmer.
Thou takest the brush – and the colours sing. So
all things have meaning and beauty in that
space beyond time where Thou art. How, then,
can I hold back anything from thee.

EVERYONE SANG

Siegfried Sassoon

Everyone suddenly burst out singing;
And I was filled with such delight
As prisoned birds must find in freedom
Winging wildly across the white
Orchards and dark green fields; on - on -
    and out of sight.

Everyone's voice was suddenly lifted;
And beauty came like the setting sun:
My heart was shaken with tears; and
    horror
Drifted away . . . O but Everyone
Was a bird; and the song was wordless;
    the singing will never be done.

SHOP

Robert Browning

Because a man has shop to mind
In time and place, since flesh must live,
Needs spirit lack all life behind,
All stray thoughts, fancies fugitive,
All loves except what trade can give?

I want to know a butcher paints,
A baker rhymes for his pursuit,
Candlestick-maker much acquaints
His soul with song, or, haply mute,
Blows out his brains upon the flute!

AN DIE MUSIK

Franz Schubert

O lovely art, in how many grey hours
When the wild round of life ensnared me
Have you kindled my heart to warm love
And carried me into a better world.

Often has a sigh, flowing from my harp,
A sweet and holy harmony from you,
Unlocked for me the heaven of better
    times.
O lovely art, I thank you for it.

UNFINISHED JOURNEY

Yehudi Menuhin

Music is given us with our existence. An infant cries, or crows or talks with his own voice and goes one step beyond to sing. Above other arts, music can be possessed without knowledge; being an expression largely of the subconscious, it has its direct routes from whatever is in our guts, minds and spirits, without need of a detour through the classroom. That direct route I knew, thank God. I learned to love music before I learned to say so; I was given the raw material when I could scarcely read or write; I early felt the wonder of taking up a violin and making it speak, communicate with others, express the thoughts and feelings of great composers. No doubt I had great aptitude which enabled me to excel my teachers in specific performances, but this phenomenon is generally accounted more mysterious than it is. Violin in hand, a talented youngster with music in his heart, an inspiring master, and the capacity to play by 'feel' and imitation can hurdle obstacles apparently insuperable to the adult mind, which would erect barriers of qualification to be surmounted before one wins the right to self-expression.

GITANJALI

Rabindranath Tagore

When thou commandest me to sing, it seems that my heart would break with pride; and I look to thy face, and tears come to my eyes.

All that is harsh and dissonant in my life melts into one sweet harmony – and my adoration spreads wings like a glad bird on its flight across the sea.

I know thou takest pleasure in my singing. I know that only as a singer I come before thy presence.

I touch by the edge of the far-spreading wing of my song thy feet which I could never aspire to reach.

Drunk with the joy of singing I forget myself and call thee friend who art my lord.

MEISTER ECKHART

R. K. Coomanoswamy

It is immaterial what the work may be, but it is essential that the artist should be wholly given to it, 'it is all the same to him what he is loving', it is working for the love of God in any case, because the perfection of the work is 'to prepare all creatures to return to God' as 'in their natural mode (they) are exemplified in divine essence', and this will hold good even if the painter paints his own portrait, God's image in himself. He is no true workman but a vainglorious showman who would astonish by his skill; 'any proper man ought to be ashamed for good people to know of this in him.'

SURPRISED BY JOY
C. S. Lewis

One other thing that Arthur taught me was to love the bodies of books. I had always respected them. My brother and I might cut up stepladders without scruple; to have thumb-marked or dog's-eared a book would have filled us with shame. But Arthur did not merely respect, he was enamoured; and soon, I too. The set up of the page, the feel and smell of the paper, the differing sounds that different papers make as you turn the leaves, became sensuous delights. This revealed to me a flaw in Kirk. How often have I shuddered when he took a new classical text of mine in his gardener's hands, bent back the boards till they creaked, and left his sign on every page.

'Yes, I remember,' said my father. 'That was old Knock's one fault.'

'A bad one,' said I.

'An all but unforgivable one,' said my father.

ON LOVE
A. R. Orage

To be in love demands that the lover shall divine the wishes of the beloved long before they have come into the beloved's own consciousness. He knows her better than she knows herself; and loves her more than she loves herself; so that she becomes her perfect self without her own conscious effort. *Her* conscious effort, when the love is mutual, is for him. Thus each delightfully works perfection in the other.

But this state is not ordinarily attained in nature: it is the fruit of art, of self-training. All people desire it, even the most cynical; but since it seldom occurs by chance, and nobody has published the key to its creation, the vast majority doubt even its possibility. Nevertheless it is possible, provided that the parties can learn and teach humbly. How to begin? Let the lover when he is about to see his beloved think what he should take, do, or say so as to give her a delightful surprise. At first it will probably be a surprise that is not a complete surprise: that is to say, she will have been aware of her wish, and only delighted that her lover had guessed it. Later the delightful surprise may really surprise her; and her remark will be: 'How did you know I should be pleased, since I should never have guessed it myself?' Constant efforts to anticipate the nascent wishes of the beloved while they are still unconscious are the means to conscious love.

ODE ON A GRECIAN URN

John Keats

Thou still unravish'd bride of quietness,
   Thou foster-child of silence and slow time,
Sylvan historian, who canst thus express
   A flowery tale more sweetly than our rhyme:
What leaf-fring'd legend haunts about thy shape
   Of deities or mortals, or of both,
      In Tempe or the dales of Arcady?
   What men or gods are these? What maidens loth?
What mad pursuit? What struggle to escape?
   What pipes and timbrels? What wild ecstasy?

Heard melodies are sweet, but those unheard
   Are sweeter; therefore, ye soft pipes, play on;
Not to the sensual ear, but, more endear'd,
   Pipe to the spirit ditties of no tone:
Fair youth, beneath the trees, thou canst not leave
   Thy song, nor ever can those trees be bare;
      Bold Lover, never, never canst thou kiss,
Though winning near the goal - yet, do not grieve;
   She cannot fade, though thou hast not thy bliss,
   For ever wilt thou love, and she be fair!

A FRIEND OF MINE

John Dawson-Reed

A friend of mine is going blind, but
    through the dimness
He sees so much better than I.
And how he cherishes each new thing
    that he sees,
They are locked in his head,
He will save them for when he's in
    darkness again.

He can't read books and he can't paint
    pictures,
But he understands so much clearer
    than I.
For he knows that all he's missing with
    his eyes is more vivid in
The mind of the man who's going blind
And that's why he doesn't mind –

Chorus
Won't you sing, Tommy Davidson, of
    things that you have seen,
Sing of winter's bite and summer nights,
And places you have been; of dew drops
    and forgetmenots,
And silver silky sheen, lain across the
    morning meadow on the hillside.

This friend of mine he plays guitar
And sings his songs so well,
And he sings so much better than I.
He can sing you any pictures in your
    mind,
He will sketch them out in rhyme, draw
    the details in the lines,
And he'll colour it in time.

And how he loves his guitar
And it loves him,
And they play so much sweeter than I
As if to say, that come the day that he
    can't see,
He will have at his command so much
    beauty in his hands,
That the loss won't come so hard.

Chorus
Won't you sing, Tommy Davidson, of
    things that you have done,
Sing of silver seagulls sailing into
    evening's golden sun,
Sing of city streets and villages and
    people on the run,
Tell the people how you know it, Tommy
    Davidson.

WHY DO I PAINT?

Brigid Marlin

Why do I paint? What is it that wells up in me and demands expression? It is very strong, and I know nothing about it; only that it has always been there. Sometimes it feels like a great longing; a longing for something that I never have had, but the mere taste of which is worth everything I have ever had. Sometimes, when I was younger, I used to try to define the feeling. 'It is like when you eat too much meat, and you long for oranges,' or, 'It is like trying to remember a tune, which you once heard; it was very beautiful and you can only remember tantalising snatches of it.' Or, 'It is like trying to trace a beautiful perfume, in a street full of different smells.'

Perhaps the analogy of the tune is best. Whenever a painting seems to be working it has the feeling of remembering the tune. The melody is always there; but I have to find my way back to it. Michelangelo put it marvellously when he said, 'The statue is always there; hidden in the block of marble. I only try to uncover it.' At one's best moments one feels that the painting was always there; and one only has to uncover it without getting in the way.

I sit at the easel and I look at what I am to paint. Now I see it as if it were for the first time. It may be a person, a scene or a still-life that I am painting, but when I look at it with attention, it begins to reveal itself to me.

For most of my waking life I lived in a sort of dream; grabbing with my eyes at what attracted me, discarding what did not, without any thought. It was only when seated before my easel that the staleness would fall from my eyes, and I would look on everything with impartial attention. This attention, this taking in of everything for what it is, is a kind of love. In this situation the painter loves the water for its wetness, the glass for its hardness, the wood for its weathered lines and cracks. No face is ugly in itself, just as no tree is ugly. We speak of attention as something that we 'give' and 'receive'; we speak of it as a gift which it is. To give attention is to create a space in myself within which the other can reveal itself to me.

When I was undergoing great personal suffering, an analogy came to me. To suffer without meaning is like being carved up by thugs; to suffer with meaning is like undergoing a necessary operation by a surgeon – even if he has not any anaesthetic, it is bearable because it has meaning.

That is why all Art is so deeply satisfying. It hints at a Meaning in the universe and gives us the hope that we are undergoing something that can be for our ultimate good, rather than just being at the mercy of random thugs.

Carpet-makers in the Orient always leave a break in the pattern somewhere; a hole in the pattern for the soul to escape through. Equally, there also should be an element of something left out or mysterious in the painting. The longing can never be satisfied completely. To try is to debase the effort of painting.

My son Christopher is a physicist; he is working on the grand theory of the unification of everything in the universe. He said that what he is basically driven by was expressed by Mother Teresa, the wish to do 'something beautiful for God'. How much more would an Artist feel this, if he were open to a belief in something higher.

CANDLES IN THE DARK

Mary Craig

[Maria Skobtsova] helped them by talking them out of their obsession with food, drawing their minds away onto a less destructive plane, talking to them of the beautiful things that man had made with his art. Many of her companions, remembers Genevieve de Gaulle, who was with her in Ravensbrück, 'sensed the presence of God in her'. In all of them 'she rekindled . . . the flame of thought which still barely flickered beneath the heavy burden of horror.' . . .

'She took us all under her wing,' said another survivor. 'We were cut off from our families; yet somehow she provided us with a family.' Maria was mother to them all, but particularly to the young Soviet women soldiers in Block 31 whom she adopted as her own, hugging them like children when they were afraid. By rights these girls were prisoners of war, but the Germans had chosen to treat them as partisans and had sent them to this concentration camp. Maria admired and loved them . . .

She was sure that the Russians would be the first on the scene to liberate them. Rosane Lascroux was equally sure that it would be the Americans and British. They took a bet on it, Maria promising a gift if Rosane should be right. When news of the Allied landings in Normandy in 1944 reached them, she kept her word, telling Rosane that she would embroider a cloth to commemorate the landings. Hidden in her mattress, Rosane had a triangular piece of white cotton which the SS had originally ordered the women to wear on their heads, but which they had later withdrawn. She was glad now that she had kept hers hidden. One of the girls, whose job it was to look after the SS shirts, found some dye; two others stole some lengths of cable from the Siemens factory where they worked; another stole a needle. All of these crimes, if discovered, would have been punishable by death.

Maria stripped the protective fabric from the cable and separated it into single threads. Standing upright on the Appel ground, supported from behind by another prisoner, Maria worked to create a thing of beauty amid such ugliness. She worked without a pattern and with scarcely a glance at the tiny corner of cloth which protruded from her striped uniform, and to which she diligently plied her needle, pushing the whole thing out of sight whenever the SS appeared. Rosane Lascroux had studied English, and she scrawled an Anglo-Saxon-type inscription in the dust, a word at a time, for Maria to copy. The finished masterpiece for which so many had risked their lives, became the greatest treasure of the women of Block 27. It depicted the arrival of the men from the north in their boats; and their victory over the evil usurpers of the land. 'Then they came, the Norsemen – the lofty fortress they besieged, and within their arms befell the rich booty. Fiercely they fought, the brave invaders, for the filthy devils were doomed to death. Meanwhile rejoiced the peaceful folk.' The Anglo-Saxon may be less than exact, but the spiritual power of this small piece of cloth is beyond measure.

ENTHUSIASMS

Bernard Levin, Sunday Times, 1983

My own love of books begins long before I start to read them. First of all, I am an incurable book-sniffer: when I open a new book I at once savour its scent, and I have had some odd looks from bookshop assistants in consequence, particularly since the next thing I do is to run my fingertips over the pages, for the sensuous pleasure to be had from touching fine book-paper is not to be underestimated. There is pleasure also to be derived from crackling a crisp page between finger and thumb; the Nonesuch Dickens, without doubt the most beautiful edition of his works ever published, has the additional advantage of being printed on paper that gives this satisfaction most intensely, and so does its baby sister, the four-volume Nonesuch Shakespeare (postwar successor to the even nobler seven-volume set), which is printed on a lovely yellow-tinged India paper. Books, though, must never be objects, and I say that with an emphasis added from a time when to me they were the most important living beings ... The source of pleasure in reading – the readability, that is, of an author – is to be found in certain qualities, and the surest clue to these qualities is the feeling we get when we meet such a writer, dead for centuries perhaps, and recognise him at once as a friend. But how do we recognise a friend? By seeing before us an open heart, and by trusting him, and ourselves, enough to enter into it. There are writers with closed hearts; this does not mean that we cannot read them, but I think it means that they cannot give us the highest pleasure of reading, for they do not offer us the love of a friend.

WHEN EARTH'S LAST PICTURE IS PAINTED

Rudyard Kipling

When Earth's last picture is painted and the tubes are twisted and dried,
When the oldest colours have faded, and the youngest critic has died,
We shall rest, and, faith, we shall need it – lie down for an æon or two,
Till the Master of All Good Workmen shall put us to work anew.

And those that were good shall be happy: they shall sit in a golden chair;
They shall splash at a ten-league canvas with brushes of comets' hair.
They shall find real saints to draw from – Magdalene, Peter, and Paul;
They shall work for an age at a sitting and never be tired at all!

And only The Master shall praise us, and only The Master shall blame;
And no one shall work for money, and no one shall work for fame,
But each for the joy of the working, and each, in his separate star,
Shall draw the Thing as he sees It for the God of Things as They are!

Love
and
Place

Love and Place

A French proverb has it that a too frequent change of one's dwelling-place wastes life. Benedict of Nursia, fifth-century founder of Western Monasticism, must have been of the same mind for so convinced was he of the spiritual advantages of staying put in the one spot that he instituted a vow of stability for his followers.

But the Scriptural view of life as a pilgrimage, and of the individual as a nomad, pitching his tent in different places, has also appealed to me; and until quite recently I felt little or no attachment to any of the places where I had hitherto lived or visited. For years I was more than content to consider myself homeless, even rootless. During my childhood, my parents moved house three times; my teenage years were spent at boarding-school and even when schooling had finished, work necessitated my being frequently on the move. There was a brief spell of living in Oxford during my engagement and in New York during my marriage, but with my widowhood the peregrinations started again, only coming to a halt with my entry into Stanbrook Abbey. Even then I had no strong sense of home as a physical place.

It was some years after my return to secular life that I happened upon the cottage in which I now live. It was here that the nesting instinct asserted itself for the first time. I named my cottage 'Rivendell' after Tolkien's *The Lord of the Rings*. It was built in 1667 by a family that had fled the London plague – which explains why they had to build the house with their own hands, unaided by the locals who feared infection. This story, if true, gives the house an added appeal to me.

Things men have made
with wakened hands and
put soft life into, are awake
through years with transferred
touch, and go on glowing
for long years. And for this
reason, some old things are
lovely, warm still with
the life of forgotten men
who made them.

Looking at the house I am reminded of those words by D. H. Lawrence. The seventeenth-century builders used old rough-hewn beams, remains of still more ancient ships, that must have plied God knows how many seas. The uneven walls and sloping floors bespeak an age very different from ours.

No matter how detached we imagine ourselves to be, I quickly discovered that even dwelling-places can become part of us. I had been living in a little flint and brick cottage kindly lent me by a friend, and at the last moment I found it inordinately difficult to move out. It took the cajoling and eventually the threats of a couple of close friends to compel me to finally leave. Gradually they had spirited away my belongings and one day they came and took with them my cooking-pots, my bed, my telephone and my harp. Could I do otherwise than follow them?

'Home', one's place, need not be purely physical, a four-walled edifice. In the Old Testament there is that deeply touching account of Ruth and Naomi. Despite the uncertainties and hardship involved in sticking with her beloved mother-in-law Naomi, the young widow Ruth insists on journeying to Bethlehem with Naomi, declaring: 'Wherever you go I will go, wherever you live I will live, your people shall be my people, and your God, my God. Wherever you die I will die and there will I be buried. May Yahweh do this thing to me and more also if even death should come between us.' No longer did Ruth consider that country of Moab her home. Her place was with Naomi. In the last analysis, however humble or unstable where the loved one is, there is home. Just as Shelley declared that familiar acts are made beautiful through love, so also places are made beautiful through love.

'Follow me where I go,' sings John Denver, 'I'd like to show you places where I'm going to, places where I've been, to have you there beside me and never be alone; and all the time you're with me, we will be at home.'

HOME-THOUGHTS, FROM ABROAD

Robert Browning

Oh, to be in England
Now that April's there,
And whoever wakes in England
Sees, some morning, unaware,
That the lowest boughs and the brushwood sheaf
Round the elm-tree bole are in tiny leaf,
While the chaffinch sings on the orchard bough
In England - now!

And after April, when May follows,
And the whitethroat builds, and all the swallows!
Hark, where my blossomed pear-tree in the hedge
Leans to the field and scatters on the clover
Blossoms and dewdrops - at the bent spray's edge -
That's the wise thrush; he sings each song twice over,
Lest you should think he never could recapture
The first fine careless rapture!

And though the fields look rough with hoary dew
All will be gay when noontide wakes anew
The buttercups, the little children's dower -
Far brighter than this gaudy melon-flower.

THE WINTER OF OUR DISCONTENT

John Steinbeck

On the edge of the silted and sanded-up Old Harbour, right where the Hawley dock had been, the stone foundation is still there. It comes right down to the low-tide level, and high water laps against its square masonry. Ten feet from the end there is a little passage about four feet wide and four feet high and five feet deep. Its top is vaulted. Maybe it was a drain one time, but the landward end is cemented in with sand and broken rock. That is my Place, the place everybody needs. Inside it you are out of sight except from seaward. There's nothing at Old Harbour now but a few clammers' shacks, rattlety things, mostly deserted in the winter, but clammers are a quiet lot anyway. They hardly speak from day's end to end and they walk with their heads down and their shoulders bowed.

That was the place I was headed for. I spent night-tide there before I went in the Service, and the night-tide before I married my Mary, and part of the night Ellen was born that hurt her so bad. I was compelled to go and sit inside there and hear the little waves slap the stone and look out at the sawtooth Whitsun rocks. I saw it, lying in bed, watching the dance of the red spots, and I knew I had to sit there. It's big changes takes me there – big changes.

South Devon runs along the shore, and there are lights aimed at the beach put there by good people to keep lovers from getting in trouble. They have to go somewhere else. A town ordinance says that Wee Willie has to patrol once an hour. There wasn't a soul on the beach – not a soul, and that was odd because someone is going fishing, or fishing, or coming in nearly all the time. I lowered myself over the edge and found the outcrop stone and doubled into the little cave. And I had hardly settled myself before I heard Wee Willie's car go by. That's twice I had avoided passing the time of night with him.

It sounds uncomfortable and silly, sitting cross-legged in a niche like a blinking Buddha, but some way the stone fits me, or I fit. Maybe I've been going there so long that my behind has conformed to the stones. As for its being silly, I don't mind that. Sometimes it's great fun to be silly, like children playing statues and dying of laughter. And sometimes being silly breaks the even pace and lets you get a new start. When I am troubled, I play a game of silly so that my dear will not catch trouble from me. She hasn't found me out yet, or if she has, I'll never know it. So many things I don't know about my Mary, and among them, how much she knows about me. I don't think she knows about the place. How could she? I've never told anyone. It has no name in my mind except the Place – no ritual or formula or anything. It's a spot in which to wonder about things. No man really knows about other human beings. The best he can do is to suppose that they are like himself. Now, sitting in the Place, out of the wind, seeing under the guardian lights the tide creep in, black from the dark sky, I wondered whether all men have a Place, or need a Place, or want one and have none. Sometimes I've seen a look in eyes, a frenzied animal look as of need for a quiet, secret place where soul shivers can abate, where a man is one and can take stock of it. Of course I know of the theories of back to the womb and the death-wish, and these may be true of some men, but I don't think they are true of me, except as easy ways of saying something that isn't easy. I call whatever happens in the Place 'taking stock'. Some others might call it prayer, and maybe it would be the same thing. I don't believe it's thought. If I wanted to make a picture of it for myself, it would be a wet sheet turning and flapping in a lovely wind and drying and sweetening the white.

THE FELLOWSHIP OF THE RING

J. R. R. Tolkien

There was a long silence. Gandalf sat down again and puffed at his pipe, as if lost in thought. His eyes seemed closed, but under the lids he was watching Frodo intently. Frodo gazed fixedly at the red embers on the hearth, until they filled all his vision, and he seemed to be looking down into profound wells of fire. He was thinking of the fabled Cracks of Doom and the terror of the Fiery Mountain.

'Well!' said Gandalf at last. 'What are you thinking about? Have you decided what to do?'

'No!' answered Frodo, coming back to himself out of darkness, and finding to his surprise that it was not dark, and that out of the window he could see the sunlit garden. 'Or perhaps, yes. As far as I understand what you have said, I suppose I must keep the Ring and guard it, at least for the present, whatever it may do to me.'

'Whatever it may do, it will be slow, slow to evil if you keep it with that purpose,' said Gandalf.

'I hope so,' said Frodo. 'But I hope that you may find some other better keeper soon. But in the meanwhile it seems that I am a danger, a danger to all that live near me. I cannot keep the Ring and stay here. I ought to leave Bag End, leave the Shire, leave everything and go away.' He sighed.

'I should like to save the Shire, if I could – though there have been times when I thought the inhabitants too stupid and dull for words, and have felt that an earthquake or an invasion of dragons might be good for them. But I don't feel like that now. I feel that as long as the Shire lies behind, safe and comfortable, I shall find wandering more bearable: I shall know that somewhere there is a firm foothold, even if my feet cannot stand there again.'

SUSSEX

Rudyard Kipling

God gave all men all earth to love,
But, since our hearts are small,
Ordained for each one spot should prove
    Beloved over all;
That, as He watched Creation's birth,
    So we, in godlike mood,
May of our love create our earth
    And see that it is good.

So one shall Baltic pines content,
    As one some Surrey glade,
Or one the palm-grove's droned lament
    Before Levuka's Trade.
Each to his choice, and I rejoice
    The lot has fallen to me
In a fair ground – in a fair ground –
    Yes, Sussex by the sea!

THE ISLAND

Sorley MacLean

O great Island, Island of my love,
many a night of them I fancied
the great ocean itself restless
agitated with love of you
as you lay on the sea,
great beautiful bird of Scotland,
your supremely beautiful wings bent
about many-nooked Loch Bracadale,
your beautiful wings prostrate on the
    sea
from the Wild Stallion to the Aird of
    Sleat,
your joyous wings spread
about Loch Snizort and the world.

O great Island, my Island, my love,
many a night I lay stretched
by your side in that slumber
when the mist of twilight swathed you.
My love every leaflet of heather on you
from Rudha Hunish to Loch Slapin,
and every leaflet of bog-myrtle kin
from Stron Bhiornaill to the Garsven,
every tarn, stream and burn a joy
from Romisdale to Brae Eynort,
and even if I came in sight of Paradise,
what price its moon without Blaven?

JOHN BETJEMAN

John Carey, Sunday Times, 1983

When Betjeman mourns for the
enormous hayfields of Perivale, or the
overtrod lanes that once rambled round
Tooting Bec, he is deliberately stimu-
lating grief, as any poet must who aims
to touch the buried springs of tenderness
in us. 'Man is in love and loves what
vanishes. What more is there to say?'
asks Yeats, unanswerably. But poets, by
making us feel for what vanishes, can
ensure that it does not quite vanish.

SONG FOR IRELAND

Phil Colclough

Walking all the day,
Near tall towers where falcons build
    their nests.
Silver winged they fly,
They know the call of freedom in their
    breasts.
Saw Black Head against the sky,
Where twisted rocks they run to the sea.

Chorus

Living on your western shore,
Saw summer sunsets, asked for more,
I stood by your Atlantic sea,
And sang a song for Ireland.

Talking all the day,
With true friends who try to make you
    stay,
Telling jokes and news,
Singing songs to pass the time away,
Watched the Galway salmon run,
Like silver, dancing, darting in the sun.

Chorus

Drinking all the day,
In old pubs where fiddlers love to play,
Saw one touch the bow,
He played a reel which seemed so grand
    and gay.
Stood on Dingle beach and cast,
In wild foam we found Atlantic bass.

Chorus

Dreaming in the night,
I see a land where no one has to fight,
Waking in your dawn,
I see you crying in the morning light,
Lying where the falcons fly,
They twist and turn all in your air blue
    sky.

Chorus

LETTER TO THE PRESIDENT OF THE UNITED STATES IN 1885

Chief Seathl

The Great Chief in Washington sends word that he wishes to buy our land. The Great Chief also sends us words of friendship and good will. This is kind of him, since we know he has little need for our friendship in return. But we will consider your offer, for we know if we do not do so, the white man may come with guns and take our land. What Chief Seathl says, the Great Chief in Washington can count on as truly as our white brothers can count on the return of the seasons. My words are like the stars – they do not set.

How can you buy or sell the sky – the warmth of the land? The idea is strange to us. Yet we do not own the freshness of the air or the sparkle of the water. How can you buy them from us? We will decide in our time.

Every part of this earth is sacred to my people. Every shining pine needle, every sandy shore, every mist in the dark woods, every clearing and humming insect is holy in the memory and experience of my people.

We know that the white man does not understand our ways. One portion of the land is the same to him as the next, for he is a stranger who comes in the night and takes from the land whatever he needs. The earth is not his brother, but his enemy, and when he has conquered it, he moves on. He leaves his fathers' graves behind and he does not care. He kidnaps the earth from his children. He does not care. His fathers' graves and his children's birthright are forgotten. His appetite will devour the earth and leave behind only a desert. The sight of your cities pains the eyes of the redman. But perhaps it is because the redman is a savage and does not understand . . .

There is no quiet place in the white man's cities. No place to hear the leaves of spring or the rustle of insects' wings. But because perhaps I am a savage and do not understand the clatter only seems to insult the ears. And what is there to life if a man cannot hear the lovely cry of the whippoorwill or the argument of the frogs around a pond at night? The Indian prefers the soft sound of the wind darting over the face of the pond, and the smell of the wind itself cleansed by a mid-day rain, or scented with pinion pine. The air is precious to the redman. For all things share the same breath – the beasts, the trees, the man. The white man does not seem to notice the air he breathes.

Like a man dying for many days, he is numb to the smell of his own stench . . . When the last redman has vanished from the earth, and the memory is only the shadow of a cloud moving across the prairie, these shores and forests will still hold the spirits of my people, for they love the earth as the newborn loves its mother's heartbeat.

If we sell you our land, love it as we've loved it. Care for it as we've cared for it. Hold in your mind the memory of the land, as it is when you take it. And with all your strength, with all your might, and with all your heart preserve it for your children, and love it as God loves us all. One thing we know – our God is the same God. This earth is precious to him. Even the white man cannot be exempt from the common destiny.

GAZING ON PRAGUE

Jaroslav Seifert

Whenever I gaze out on Prague
- and I do so constantly and always
with bated breath
    because I love her –
I turn my mind to God
wherever he may be,
    beyond the starry mists or just behind
that moth-eaten screen,
    to thank him
    for granting that magnificent setting
to me to live in.
To me and to my joys and carefree
loves,
    to me and to my tears without
weeping
    when the loves departed,
    and to my more-than-bitter grief
    when even my verses could not weep.
I love her fire-charred walls
    to which we clung during the war

so as to hold out.
    I would not change them for anything
in the world.
    Not even for others.
    Not even if the Eiffel tower rose
between them
    and the Seine flowed sadly past,
    not even for all the gardens of
paradise
    full of flowers.
    When I shall die - and this will be
quite soon -
    I shall still carry on my heart this
city's destiny.
    And mercilessly, just as Marsyas, let
anyone be flayed alive
    who lays hands on this city,
    no matter who he is.
    No matter how sweetly he plays
    on his flute.

AN OLD WOMAN OF THE ROADS

Padraic Colum

O, to have a little house!
To own the hearth and stool and all!
The heaped up sods upon the fire,
The pile of turf against the wall!

To have a clock with weights and chains
And pendulum swinging up and down!
A dresser filled with shining delph,
Speckled and white and blue and
    brown!

I could be busy all the day
Clearing and sweeping hearth and floor,
And fixing on their shelf again
My white and blue and speckled store!

I could be quiet there at night
Beside the fire and by myself,
Sure of a bed and loth to leave
The ticking clock and the shining delph!

Och! but I'm weary of mist and dark,
And roads where there's never a house
    nor bush,
And tired I am of bog and road,
And the crying wind and the lonesome
    hush!

And I am praying to God on high,
And I am praying Him night and day,
For a little house - a house of my own -
Out of the wind's and the rain's way.

THE OLD VICARAGE, GRANTCHESTER

Rupert Brooke

Ah God! to see the branches stir
Across the moon at Grantchester!
To smell the thrilling-sweet and rotten
Unforgettable, unforgotten
River-smell, and hear the breeze
Sobbing in the little trees.
Say, do the elm-clumps greatly stand
Still guardians of that holy land?
The chestnuts shade, in reverend dream,
The yet unacademic stream?
Is dawn a secret shy and cold
Anadyomene, silver-gold?
And sunset still a golden sea
From Haslingfield to Madingley?
And after, ere the night is born,
Do hares come out about the corn?
Oh, is the water sweet and cool,
Gentle and brown, above the pool?
And laughs the immortal river still
Under the mill, under the mill?
Say, is there Beauty yet to find?
And Certainty? and Quiet kind?
Deep meadows yet, for to forget
The lies, and truths, and pain? ... oh! yet
Stands the Church clock at ten to three?
And is there honey still for tea?

THE LAY OF THE LAST MINSTREL

Sir Walter Scott

Breathes there a man with soul so dead,
Who never to himself hath said,
This is my own, my native land!
Whose heart hath ne'er within him
    burn'd
As home his footsteps he hath turn'd
From wandering on a foreign strand!

GOD'S PROMISE TO DAVID
Psalm 132

O Lord, remember David
and all the hardships he endured,
the oath he swore to the Lord,
his vow to the Strong One of Jacob.

'I will not enter the house where I live
nor go to the bed where I rest.
I will give no sleep to my eyes,
to my eyelids will give no slumber
till I find a place for the Lord,
a dwelling for the Strong One of Jacob.'

At Ephrata we heard of the ark;
we found it in the plains of Yearim.
'Let us go to the place of his dwelling;
let us go to kneel at his footstool.'

Go up, Lord, to the place of your rest,
you and the ark of your strength.
Your priests shall be clothed with
    holiness:
your faithful shall ring out their joy...

For the Lord has chosen Sion;
he has desired it for his dwelling:
'This is my resting-place for ever,
here have I chosen to live.'

HARLEQUIN
Morris West

I walked out into the sunshine, took a taxi to the Tidal Basin, leisurely as any provincial tourist, to commune with old Thomas Jefferson in his shrine among the cherry trees.

I will tell you a sentimental secret. This is one place in America which I truly love. This is one man in all her turbulent history who moves me to admiration and, all too rarely, to meditation. Scraps and snippets of his wise and tolerant code sound longer in my memory than the strident voices of my own time. He hated 'the morbid rage of debate'. 'If I could not get to heaven but with a party, I would not go there at all ... Some men look at constitutions with sanctimonious reverence and deem them, like the ark of the covenant, too sacred to be touched...' I suppose that, younger and more open, I had seen in him what I had found – and lost – in George Harlequin: a largeness of mind, wit, humour and a soul hospitable to the whole experience of mankind.

Even so early, there were lovers and families on the lawns and I envied them. I was grateful that the shrine was empty, so that I could brood in the solitude of the past, which is like the solitude of the sea, cleansing and healing.

LOVE IS A PLACE
E. E. Cummings

love is a place
and through this place of
love move
(with brightness of peace)
all places.

NUPTIALS

Albert Camus

To the left of the port, a stairway of dry stones leads to the ruins, through the mastic-trees and broom. The path goes in front of the small lighthouse before plunging into the open country. Already, at the foot of this lighthouse, large red and yellow cactus plants go down towards the first rocks sucked at by the kissing sound of the sea. As we stand in the slight breeze, with the sun warming one side of our faces, we watch the light coming down from the sky, the smooth sea smiling with its glittering teeth. Before entering the ruins' kingdom, we stand for the last time as mere spectators.

After a few steps, the smell of absinthe seizes you by the throat. Their grey wool covers the ruins as far as the eye can see. Their oil ferments in the heat, and the whole earth gives off a heady alcohol which makes the sky quiver. We stride to the meeting-place of love and desire. We are not seeking lessons or the bitter philosophy required from greatness. Nothing matters here but the sun, kisses and the wild scents of the earth. I myself do not seek to be alone there. I have often been there with those I loved and read on their features the clear smile taken by the face of love. Here, I leave others to concern themselves with order and with moderation. The great free love of nature and the sea absorbs me completely. In this marriage between ruins and springtime, the ruins have become stones again, and, losing the polish imposed on them by men, have gone back to nature. Nature has celebrated the return of these prodigal daughters by laying out a profusion of flowers. The heliotrope pushes its red and white head between the flagstones of the forum, and red geraniums spill their blood over what were houses, temples and public squares. Like those men whom much knowledge brings back to God, many years have brought these ruins back to their mother's house. Today, their past has finally left them, and nothing distracts them from that deep force which draws them back to the centre of the things which fall.

ISLAND MOON

Agnes Mure Mackenzie

Tonight there is a restlessness in the wind,
There is small rain that has salt in it from the sea
And the white breakers wander in the dark.

Low down in the West a waning moon calls to the sea,
Sweeping back the flood from the black points of land
And the tide is turning from the Seven Rocks.

Perhaps the moon is shining for you in the far country?
But the skies there are not Island skies!
You will not remember the salt smell of the sea and the little rain.

The smell of the night is rising from the land –
Wet grass and breath of kine, and salt and blue smoke
That drifts inland on the restlessness of the wind.

And the trouble in me goes out on the wind like smoke
Only it goes against the wind far out into the far country
Where you are, beyond the black line of the sea.

IN PLEASANT PLACES

Joyce Grenfell

By 'magic' I don't mean abracadabra and fairy godmothers with wishes, nor do I mean witches and spells and funny goings on at seances.

I mean the heightened quality of certain, often quite small, experiences lit by unexplained excitement, powerful with innocence. It can come from looking hard at a shell, arriving at an unexpected view of the sea, hearing a bar of music.

> To see a World in a Grain of Sand,
> And a Heaven in a Wild Flower,
> Hold Infinity in the palm of your hand,
> And Eternity in an hour.

Some of my contemporaries don't agree with me that this kind of magic is far more potent in middle age than when one was new. It is so for me because now I bring more to each experience, and 'magic' is very nourishing.

Places induce it. East Anglia. The bush in Australia. I get it particularly in a certain small valley in Cumberland. The first time I went there, having chosen a place to stay from an unillustrated guide-book with just an inch of unexaggerated prose, we drove across a high bare pass and as we came near it I knew – this is it! I said it out loud, too. It was recognition, and I get it unfailingly every time I go back there. (I get it whenever I make a new discovery of *anything*.) I don't think I knew what people meant when they said a place was their spiritual home. But I do now.

AT THE MID HOUR OF NIGHT

Thomas Moore

At the mid hour of night, when stars are weeping, I fly
To the lone vale we loved, when life shone warm in thine eye;
    And I think that if spirits can steal from the regions of air,
    To revisit past scenes of delight, thou wilt come to me there,
And tell me our love is remember'd even in the sky!
Then I sing the wild song it once was rapture to hear,
When our voices, commingling, breathed like one, on the ear;
    And, as Echo far off through the vale my sad orison rolls,
    I think, O my love! 'tis thy voice from the Kingdom of Souls,
Faintly answering still the notes that once were so clear.

BOTHY IN THE WOOD

Anon

I have a bothy in the wood –
none knows it save the Lord my God;
one wall an ash the other hazel
and a great fern makes the door.

The door posts are made of heather,
the lintel of honeysuckle;
and wild forest all around
yields mast for well-fed swine.

This size my hut: the smallest thing,
homestead amid well-trod paths;
a woman (but blackbird clothed and
    seeming)
warbles sweetly from its gable.

This little secret humble place
holds tenure of the teeming woods,
may be you will come to see?
but alone I live quite happy.

THE LAKE ISLE OF INNISFREE

W. B. Yeats

I will arise and go now, and go to
    Innisfree,
And a small cabin build there, of clay
    and wattles made:
Nine bean-rows will I have there,
    a hive for the honeybee,
And live alone in the bee-loud
    glade.

And I shall have some peace there,
    for peace comes dropping slow,
Dropping from the veils of the morning
    to where the cricket sings;
There midnight's all a glimmer,
    and noon a purple glow,
And evening full of the linnet's
    wings.

I will arise and go now, for always
    night and day
I hear lake water lapping with low
    sounds by the shore;
While I stand on the roadway, or
    on the pavements grey,
I hear it in the deep heart's core.

AFTON WATER

Robert Burns

Flow gently, sweet Afton, among thy green braes,
Flow gently, I'll sing thee a song in thy praise;
My Mary's asleep by thy murmuring stream,
Flow gently, sweet Afton, disturb not her dream.

Thou stock dove whose echo resounds thro' the glen,
Ye wild whistling blackbirds in yon thorny den,
Thou green crested lapwing thy screaming forbear,
I charge you disturb not my slumbering Fair.

How lofty, sweet Afton, thy neighbouring hills,
Far mar'k with the courses of clear, winding rills;
There daily I wander as noon rises high,
My flocks and my Mary's sweet Cot in my eye.

How pleasant thy banks and green vallies below,
Where wild in the woodlands the primroses blow;
There oft as mild ev'ning weeps over the lea,
The sweet scented birch shades my Mary and me.

Flow gently, sweet Afton, among thy green braes,
Flow gently, sweet River, the theme of my lays;
My Mary's asleep by thy murmuring stream,
Flow gently, sweet Afton, disturb not her dream.

NOT WHOLLY IN THE BUSY WORLD

Alfred Lord Tennyson

Not wholly in the busy world, nor quite
Beyond it, blooms the garden that I love.
News from the humming city comes to it
In sound of funeral or of marriage bells;
And, sitting muffled in dark leaves, you hear
The windy clanging of the minster clock;
Although between it and the garden lies
A league of grass, wash'd by a slow broad stream,
That, stirr'd with languid pulses of the oar,
Waves all its lazy lilies, and creeps on,
Barge-laden, to three arches of a bridge
Crown'd with the minster-towers.
The fields between
Are dewy-fresh, browsed by deep-udder'd kine,
And all about the large lime feathers low,
The lime a summer home of murmurous wings.

VENTURE TO THE INTERIOR

Laurens van der Post

Suddenly both Quillan and I heard voices, European voices. Although we could distinguish no words, the conversation sounded so close that we stopped and looked round us. At first we could see nothing, but the voices went on in a tone and a manner that suggested a happy, untroubled domestic Saturday afternoon conversation. I could hardly credit my senses, but the voices were those of the Vances down in the valley, nearly a mile away [looking] for all the world as if they were alone in Kensington Gardens on a Saturday afternoon instead of on a wild mountain top in Central Africa. I must admit I thought it a strikingly incongruous sight and I said to Quillan:

'You know they behave as if Chambe were their own private and personal suburb.'

'Yes, I know,' he answered, and smiled. 'They do look thoroughly at home. You wouldn't think that less than a year ago she had never seen Africa and he only knew it very slightly...

'Only this morning Val asked me never to move them anywhere else. When I said we would have to in two years' time when Dicky was promoted, she answered dis-dainfully, "Oh, that! We do not want to be promoted. Dicky and I have talked it over again and again, and we both want to stay here for ever." It is rather wonderful, isn't it?'

Indeed, I agreed it was wonderful; and yet I had reservations, not perhaps so much on the Vances' score, as on Africa's unpredictable account. I am at heart too much of a nomad to trust and understand love of just one place, particularly one African place. I am sure one cannot love life enough; but I believe, too, one mustn't confuse love of life with the love of certain things in it. One cannot pick the moment and place as one pleases and say, 'Enough! This is all I want. This is how it is henceforth to be.' That sort of present betrays past and future. Life is its own journey; pre-supposes its own change and movement, and one tries to arrest them at one's eternal peril. As I listened to Quillan, I just hoped fervently that this most unsuburban of mountains felt about it all as the Vances did.

'If one lived here long,' I told him, 'I believe one would have to appease the mountain in some big way. I believe one would have to become a Druid of sorts and build stone altars and sacrifice live leopards on cedar coals to its spirit.'

Quillan roared with laughter and said that often in the forests in the hills of Cyprus he felt if only he could pull the boots off the shepherds he would find that they had not human but goat's feet. And on that note we went down to the hut and the Vances.

Love
and
Romance

Love and Romance

The one riddle, the one great enterprise in
this world,
Is to learn how to love and keep loving.

———————

Each time I read them I am struck anew by
the truth of those words from a poem by my
late husband Richard Selig. Life is indeed one
ceaseless exploration and adventure in learn-
ing about loving. Love is what makes the
human condition tolerable. Joyce Cary once
wrote: 'Love doesn't grow on the trees like
apples in Eden – it's something you have to
make. And you have to use your imagination
to make it, too, just like anything else. It's all
work, work.' It is give and it is take and in this
instance I am not altogether sure that it is
more blessed to give than to receive.
Ladislaus Boros wrote that the love that
receives can be as great as the love that
gives. An old Gaelic proverb has it that 'a
person who has not loved is like a candle that
has not been lit' and that 'a candle loses
nothing of its own light by lighting another'.
Comparisons between love and light are
frequent in literature, a most comforting
simile. Vincent van Gogh voices the same
idea: 'There is the same difference in a
person before and after he is in love as
between an unlighted lamp and one that is
burning. The lamp was there and was a good
lamp but now it sheds light too and that is its
real function.'

In his scholarly work *The Allegory of Love*,
C. S. Lewis pointed out the contrast between
romantic or courtly love and that of the
Christian ideal. The romantic love he wrote
about first appeared in the literature of the
eleventh century, making its poetic entrance
in Provence. The romantic love of today,
though somewhat different in its manifestation, is its direct descendant and still makes
good copy. Furthermore, thank heavens, the
two don't necessarily clash.

As far as I can recall, my own earliest
experience of romantic love was of the
unrequited variety. As a child and adolescent I
was afflicted with an almost crippling
shyness which prevented me from expressing any amorous feelings I may have had
towards the opposite sex. I had my first
'crush' at the age of about eight. The un-
witting object was a small boy whom I had to
agonise about from afar because he was a
member not of my brother's but of a rival
'gang'. Such was his effect on me that one
Sunday morning when he sat with his family
in the seat behind me in church, I was so
distracted that Mass was almost over before
I realised that I had been holding my prayer
book upside down.

During a recent concert tour of Canada I
bumped into Gráinne Hession, a childhood
neighbour, and we spent a most pleasant
evening reminiscing about our other even
earlier childhood 'crushes'. There was four-
year-old Dennis who assiduously collected
the cardboard tops of milk bottles and left
them every Saturday at my back door with
the touching message, 'money-cows for
Maly'. He never got thanked for them (I
always avoided being around at delivery
times) for his advances were not at all
welcome – my three-year-old heart spurned
him. Gráinne vividly recalls our somewhat
cavalier treatment of two other local boys
who were very keen on us. On the way home
from school together Gráinne and I used to
walk hand in hand through a daisy-covered
field and sit ourselves on a big rock in the
middle of it. From our perch we commanded
our suitors to catch in a jar the butterflies of
our fancy. Then we'd scold the pair of them
for hurting the beautiful creatures and
demand that they release them immediately.
They just couldn't win, those ardent five-
year-old wooers. So much for the beginnings
of romantic love.

THE LONELY

Paul Gallico

There was a heavy rumbling, and a dim, flickering eye pierced the darkness as the bus charged around the corner and screeched to a halt. The waiting line stirred and shifted, and in another instant the face of Patches would have vanished from the shaft of light, when Jerry sprang forward, shouting her name: 'Patches! Patches!' And as she turned at the familiar and so desperately longed-for sound of his voice, he reached her side and swept her into his arms, and held her there tightly, all wet and cold and shivery, as she had been once before, the night they were lost on the moors.

The bus conductor shouted: 'Come along now!' The line surged onward, pushing and scrambling to board the bus. No one looked, or stopped or bothered to notice the American flyer and the little WAAF with the white face who had been there a moment ago, for the darkness had swallowed them up.

They were together in each other's arms in a niche beneath a small stone gate-arch at the top of an alley, and Jerry held Patches close to him, saying: 'Patches . . . Patches, I love you so . . .'

He could not get enough of holding her so closely that he could feel her heart pounding deep beneath her clothes, of kissing her eyes, her mouth, her temples, even the damp cloth of her uniform because it was a part of her, of touching her face with his fingers, exploring her features, saying over and over that he loved her, as though in one torrential outburst he could make up to her all that he had once denied.

As though she had been lost to him for years instead of days he cried: 'Patches, I've found you . . . I love you . . . Will you marry me, Patches . . . please, dear Patches?'

And Patches knew only that she was safe in Jerry's arms, sobbing: 'Oh, Jerry, don't let me go. Don't ever leave me again,' and that for the throbbing moment the darkness was lifted for her too. There had been no chance for her to think, to prepare herself. She did not know whence he had come or how he had found her, but only that she was in his arms, calling his name, answering his every desire for contact with her, giving him her mouth and her eyes wet with tears and rain, holding his face cupped in her hands, straining her body to his so that it might never be torn away, making little sounds in her throat at each renewed touch of his lips or his hands, listening with her heart's blood to him saying that he loved her.

She was so parched and starved for the things he was telling her, the husky, broken sentences of love, that she was hearing him with her soul, soaking it up as a thirsty flower does the rain after a drought, and there in the darkness, clinging to him, her head pressed hard against his chest, as though she would lay her cheek against his heart, she began to live again, to swell with singing joy and happiness. The black abyss that had threatened to engulf her had closed; sweet earth upheld her feet again.

'Patches, I love you . . .'

'I love you, Jerry. Forever . . . .'

'Will you marry me, Patches? You haven't said . . .'

'Yes, Jerry. I will.'

A SEVERE MERCY

Sheldon Vanauken

... in January one of us found something on falling in love that, with the appropriate pronouns, was just the way it was for both of us. A bit sentimental, perhaps, but then lovers are. It is quoted from memory, perhaps inaccurately, with thanks to the unknown author:

> To hold her in my arms against the twilight and be her comrade for ever – this was all I wanted so long as my life should last ... And this, I told myself with a kind of wonder, this was what love was: this consecration, this curious uplifting, this sudden inexplicable joy, and this intolerable pain.

What was happening was happening to us both. I believe it is always so, mutual and, at least at first, equally intense, if it is genuine inloveness. The actual thing – inloveness – requires something like a spark leaping back and forth from one to the other becoming more intense every moment, love building up like voltage in a coil. Here there is no sound of one hand clapping. Unreciprocated love is something else, not genuine inloveness, I think: perhaps it is infatuation and passion or, perhaps, potential inloveness. I believe that genuine inloveness is rather less common than the romantic novelists suggest. One who has never been in love might mistake either infatuation or a mixture of affection and sexual attraction for being in love. But when the 'real thing' happens, there is no doubt. A man in the jungle at night, as someone said, may suppose a hyena's growl to be a lion's; but when he hears the lion's growl, he knows damn' well it's a lion. So with the genuine inloveness. So with Davy and me. A sudden glory.

SUMMUM BONUM

Robert Browning

All the breath and the bloom of the year
    in the bag of one bee:
All the wonder and wealth of the mine in
    the heart of one gem:
In the core of one pearl all the shade and
    the shine of the sea:
Breath and bloom, shade and shine, -
wonder, wealth, and - how far above
    them -
Truth, that's brighter than gem,
Trust, that's purer than pearl, -
Brightest truth, purest trust in the
    universe - all were for me
In the kiss of one girl.

ARCADIA

Sir Philip Sidney

My true love hath my heart, and I have
    his,
By just exchange, one for the other
    giv'n.
I hold his dear, and mine he cannot
    miss:
There never was a better bargain driv'n.

His heart in me, keeps me and him in
    one,
My heart in him, his thoughts and
    senses guides:
He loves my heart, for once it was his
    own:
I cherish his, because in me it bides.

His heart his wound received from my
    sight:
My heart was wounded with his
    wounded heart,
For as from me, on him his hurt did
    light,
So still methought in me his hurt did
    smart:
Both equal hurt, in this change sought
    our bliss:
My true love hath my heart and I have
    his.

SILENT NOON

Dante Gabriel Rossetti

Your hands lie open in the long
    fresh grass, -
    The finger-points look through like
      rosy blooms:
    Your eyes smile peace. The pasture
      gleams and glooms
'Neath billowing skies that scatter and
    amass.

All round our nest, far as the eye can
    pass,
    Are golden kingcup-fields with silver
      edge
    Where the cow-parsley skirts the
      hawthorn-hedge.
'Tis visible silence, still as the hour-glass.

Deep in the sun-searched growths the
    dragon-fly
    Hangs like a blue thread loosened
      from the sky:
    So this wing'd hour is dropt to us
      from above.
Oh! clasp we to our hearts, for deathless
    dower,
This close-companioned inarticulate
    hour
    When twofold silence was the song of
      love.

MY HEART WAS AN ABANDONED HOUSE

Rosemary Davies

My heart was an abandoned house, refusing all repairs,
So many months of weeping had washed away the stairs,
Nothing moved the dust and ashes scattered on the floor,
I'd left a No Admittance warning hanging on the door.

You opened wide a window,
Let in a gentle breeze,
The scent of hidden blossom
And a murmuring of bees.

My heart was crouched in darkness, aching with the cold,
I curled inside the hardness, my heart was growing old,
What lover could draw near it to cast the pain aside,
The temperature was zero, by morn he would have died.

You opened wide a window,
Let in new rain, new moons,
The sound of distant singing
And a drift of white balloons.

My heart leapt out of silence, it heard remembered airs,
They opened doors and windows and built a flight of stairs,
The songs blew round and round my house, the icy winds blew out,
The sun spilled in like laughter, cast out my dark and doubt.

You opened wide a window,
I came to meet you there,
You carried small red roses
To plait into my hair.

A RED, RED ROSE

Robert Burns

O my Luve's like a red, red rose
That's newly sprung in June:
O my Luve's like the melodie
That's sweetly play'd in tune.

As fair art thou, my bonnie lass,
So deep in luve am I:
And I will luve thee still, my dear,
Till a' the seas gang dry:

Till a' the seas gang dry, my dear,
And the rocks melt wi' the sun;
I will luve thee still, my dear,
While the sands o' life shall run.

And fare thee weel, my only Luve!
And fare thee weel a while!
And I will come again, my Luve,
Tho' it were ten thousand mile.

FAR FROM THE MADDING CROWD

Thomas Hardy

The only superiority in women that is tolerable to the rival sex is, as a rule, that of the unconscious kind; but a superiority which recognizes itself may sometimes please by suggesting possibilities of capture to the subordinated man.

This well-favoured and comely girl soon made appreciable inroads upon the emotional constitution of young Farmer Oak.

Love being an extremely exacting usurer (a sense of exorbitant profit, spiritually, by an exchange of hearts, being at the bottom of pure passions, as that of exorbitant profit, bodily or materially, is at the bottom of those of lower atmosphere), every morning Oak's feelings were as sensitive as the money-market in calculations upon his chances. His dog waited for his meals in a way so like that in which Oak waited for the girl's presence that the farmer was quite struck with the resemblance, felt it lowering, and would not look at the dog. However, he continued to watch through the hedge for her regular coming, and thus his sentiments towards her were deepened without any corresponding effect being produced upon herself. Oak had nothing finished and ready to say as yet, and not being able to frame love phrases which end where they begin; passionate tales –

– Full of sound and fury
– Signifying nothing –

he said no word at all.

By making inquiries he found that the girl's name was Bathsheba Everdene . . . Gabriel had reached a pitch of existence he never could have anticipated a short time before. He liked saying 'Bathsheba' as a private enjoyment instead of whistling; turned over his taste to black hair, though he had sworn by brown ever since he was a boy, isolated himself till the space he filled in the public eye was contemptibly small. Love is a possible strength in an actual weakness. Marriage transforms a distraction into a support, the power of which should be, and happily often is, in direct proportion to the degree of imbecility it supplants. Oak began now to see light in this direction, and said to himself, 'I'll make her my wife, or upon my soul I shall be good for nothing!'

BURKE STREET

George Scott Moncrieff

One of those nights dominates in memory, pushing out all the others until they are only part of the background to that night on which I fell in love. It was hardly the first time, and it was certainly not the last. Yet it remains the most poignant and memorable of all those doomful occasions that used to rack my life so irresistibly, with unrealizable hopes and inescapable despondencies. There have been countless efforts to analyse the process of falling in love and there will be countless more again. Certainly, when one is much older, if one has allowed oneself to grow up, it all seems much plainer and more comprehensible. Yet a thrilling mystery remains. Only the devotees of the 'psychological approach' hope to exorcise it by recording self-evident elements in a jargon that makes them banal and therefore inept, untrue since the reality is never banal and is therefore simply inexpressible in terms of pseudo-scientific dullness even when, to reintroduce some sense of the mystery it has rejected, it concludes by making appeal to myth. To some degree, of course, the reality is simple: it occupies a gap already there, a predilection that is something fine, real, pursuing-of-truth, in the young, but becomes rather tattered and jaded, less truthful, as one grows older and to indulge one's emotions has to turn an ever deafer ear to experience. At the worst it may at last become entirely an emotional indulgence decked out and sustained by imaginings for whose justification one must feverishly lie to oneself.

But when one is young it is different. It is not false then to suppose that this may be the road to heaven: for that is just what it can be, or at least a high part of that road, and the more so the more that the very idealistic element that most frightens one is allowed to dominate. Of course the idealism is wrapped about with all sorts of tinsel ornament, which somehow, then or long after, must be shed, or put away like a faded bouquet only occasionally to be brought out with a brief and gentle sigh.

My predispositions were plain enough: my young manhood, with an accompanying, hardly uncommon, loneliness: my enthusiasm for things Scottish and romantic pride in my Highland ancestry: even my aesthetic sensibility. I came into Mrs Murphy's parlour rather late one evening when the room was already thick and clamorous, to find three strangers in the company. I quickly learnt, for he was taking a leading part in the conversation, that the man was called Hans, and from his accent that he was a German: the two girls were apparently of his party. They were both attractive, the one rather small and dark, the other taller, fuller, obviously the younger. They had a distinctive cast of countenance of the kind that makes one suspect a person of being a foreigner and for some time I assumed that they also were Germans although their looks were by no means Teutonic. Then Hans appealed loudly to 'my wife', and the darker girl spoke, in an accent I could not immediately place. 'No, no,' she said, 'not me. Ask Margaret. Margaret will.'

Hans turned to the second girl: 'You sing it, Margaret.'

'Go on, Margaret,' urged the dark girl, 'sing it – you know, the one you sang last night.'

At that moment Margaret established herself absolutely in my awareness. It was not only that she asked simply, 'Shall I stand up?' without bashfulness, feigned or real, yet without seeming to push herself forward: but she carried a beauty and character in her face and person that suggested that she held an answer to the million unspoken questions of my youthfulness. . . . It was the first time I had ever heard a traditional Gaelic song properly sung, and with it Margaret stepped into my predispositions, filling them with a wild overflowing.

Margaret's voice, although small, was lovely, and her expression exquisite. There was tremendous enthusiasm when she had finished.

Margaret sang again, and again I was caught in a surge of identification, that wonderful liberation from self which is the fundamental yearning of man, intrinsic to falling in love or to art just as it is, on its lowest level, to inebriation, or, on its highest, to religion.

I was brash, rather shy, little at ease with girls, but somehow I reached her side and blurted out, 'That was wonderful – the way you sang!'

She looked at me with candid grey eyes. 'You liked it?' she said. 'Who are you?'

If her interest overjoyed me, her absolute ease and calm composed me, I no longer blurted but spoke with an ease outside myself. 'My name's Ian Cameron,' I said. 'Where do you live?'

LOVE POEM

John Frederick Nims

My clumsiest dear, whose hands
   shipwreck vases,
At whose quick touch all glasses chip
   and ring,
Whose palms are bulls in china, burs in
   linen,
And have no cunning with any soft
   thing.

Except all ill-at-ease fidgeting people:
The refugee uncertain at the door
You make at home; deftly you steady
The drunk clambering on his undulant
   floor.

Unpredictable dear, the taxi drivers'
   terror,
Shrinking from far headlights pale as a
   dime
Yet leaping before red apoplectic
   streetcars –

Misfit in any space. And never on time.

A wrench in clocks and the solar system.
   Only
With words and people and love you
   move at ease.
In traffic of wit expertly manoeuvre
And keep us, all devotion, at your knees.

Forgetting your coffee spreading on our
   flannel,
Your lipstick grinning on our coat,
So gaily in love's unbreakable heaven
Our souls on glory of spilt bourbon float.

Be with me, darling, early and late.
   Smash glasses –
I will study wry music for your sake.
For should your hands drop white and
   empty
All the toys of the world would break.

THE BLACK PRINCE

Iris Murdoch

I had in fact lived through almost the whole history of 'being in love' in just over two days. (I say 'almost the whole history' because there is yet more to come.) The condensed phenomenology of the business had been enacted within me. On the first day I was simply a saint. I was so warmed and vitalized by sheer gratitude that I overflowed with charity. I felt so privileged and glorified that resentment, even memory of any wrong done to me seemed inconceivable. I wanted to go around touching people, blessing them, communicating my great happiness, the good news, the *secret* of how the whole universe was a place of joy and freedom filled and running over with selfless rapture. I did not even want to see Julian on that day. I did not even need her. It was enough to know that she existed. I could *almost* have forgotten her, as perhaps the mystic forgets God, when he becomes God.

On the second day I began to need her, though even 'anxiety' would be too gross a word for that delicate silken magnetic tug as it manifested itself at any rate initially. Self was reviving. On the first day Julian had been everywhere. On the second day, absent. This inspired the small craving for strategy, a little questing desire to make plans. The future, formerly blotted out by an excess of light, reappeared. There were once more vistas, hypotheses, possibilities. But joy and gratitude still lightened the world and made possible a gentle concern with other people, other things. I wonder how long a man could remain in that first phase of love? Much longer than I did, no doubt, but surely not indefinitely. The second phase, I am sure, given favourable conditions, could continue much longer. (But again, not indefinitely. Love is history, is dialectic, it *must* move.) As it is, I lived in hours what another man might have lived in years.

The transformation of my beatitude could, as that second day wore on, be measured by a literally physical sense of strain, as if magnetic rays or even ropes or chains were delicately plucking, then tugging, then dragging. Physical desire had of course been with me from the first, but earlier it had been, though perceptually localized, metaphysically diffused into a general glory. Sex is our great connection with the world, and at its most felicitous and spiritual it is no servitude since it informs everything and enables us to inhabit and enjoy all that we touch and look upon. At other times it settles in the body like a toad. It becomes a drag, a weight: not necessarily for this reason unwelcome. We may love our chains and our stripes too. By the time Julian telephoned I was in deep anxiety and yearning but not in hell. I could not then willingly have put off seeing her, the craving was too acute. But I was able, when I was with her, to be perfectly happy. I did not expect the inferno.

LAUNCELOT WITH BICYCLE

Phyllis McGinley

Her window looks upon the lane.
From it, anonymous and shy,
Twice daily she can see him plain,
Wheeling heroic by.
She droops her cheek against the pane
And gives a little sigh.

Above him maples at their bloom
Shake April pollen down like stars
While he goes whistling past her room
Toward unimagined wars,
A tennis visor for his plume,
Scornful of handlebars.

And, counting over in her mind
His favors, gleaned like windfall fruit
(A morning when he spoke her kind,
An afterschool salute,
A number that she helped him find,
Once, for his paper route),

Sadly she twists a stubby braid
And closer to the casement leans –
A wistful and a lily maid
In moccasins and jeans,
Despairing from the seventh grade
To match his lordly teens.

And so she grieves in Astolat
(Where other girls have grieved the
    same)
For being young and therefore not
Sufficient to his fame –
Who will by summer have forgot
Grief, April, and his name.

STRAWBERRIES

Edwin Morgan

There were never strawberries
like the ones we had
that sultry afternoon
sitting on the step
of the open french window
facing each other
your knees held in mine
the blue plates on our laps
the strawberries glistening
in the hot sunlight
we dipped them in sugar
looking at each other
not hurrying the feast
for one to come
the empty plates
laid on the stone together
with the two forks crossed
and I bent towards you
sweet in that air
in my arms
abandoned like a child
from your eager mouth
the taste of strawberries
in my memory
lean back again
let me love you

let the sun beat
on our forgetfulness
one hour of all
the heat intense
and summer lightning
on the Kilpatrick hills

let the storm wash the plates

SOLDIER

Eleanor Farjeon

I walked in my clogs on Salisbury Plain,
And all of a sudden it started to rain!
The Plain was as broad as the Plain was bare,
There wasn't an inch of shelter there.

As I was wondering what to do
Before my petticoat got wet through,
All of a sudden a Soldier came -
'Corporal Caramel is my name.

'I've a waterproof tent of a lovely green
That will keep you dry in this dripping scene.'
All of a sudden I upped and went
To Corporal Caramel's waterproof tent.

He sat me down on a rubbery sheet,
Took off my clogs and dried my feet.
He looked so stalwart, he looked so smart,
All of a sudden I lost my heart.

He dried my feet and put on my clogs,
And said, 'It is raining cats and dogs!
Why don't you stay and be my wife?'
So all of a sudden I stayed for life.

THE CONFIRMATION

Edwin Muir

Yes, yours, my love, is the right human face.
I in my mind had waited for this long,
Seeing the false and searching for the true,
Then found you as a traveller finds a place
Of welcome suddenly amid the wrong
Valleys and rocks and twisting roads. But you,
What shall I call you? A fountain in a waste,
A well of water in a country dry,
Or anything that's honest and good, an eye
That makes the whole world bright. Your open heart,
Simple with giving, gives the primal deed,
The first good world, the blossom, the blowing seed,
The hearth, the steadfast land, the wandering sea,
Not beautiful or rare in every part,
But like yourself, as they were meant to be.

PSYCHOLOGICAL REFLECTIONS

C. G. Jung

If you take a typical intellectual who is terribly afraid of falling in love, you will think his fear very foolish. But he is most probably right, because he will very likely make foolish nonsense when he falls in love. He will be caught most certainly, because his feeling only reacts to an archaic or to a dangerous type of woman. This is why many intellectuals are inclined to marry beneath them. They are caught by the landlady perhaps, or by the cook, because they are unaware of their archaic feeling through which they get caught. But they are right to be afraid, because their undoing will be in their feeling. Nobody can attack them in their intellect. There they are strong and can stand alone, but in their feelings they can be influenced, they can be caught, they can be cheated, and they know it. Therefore never force a man into his feeling when he is an intellectual. He controls it with an iron hand because it is very dangerous.

WILLIE'S GANE TAE MELVILLE CASTLE

Anon

Oh Willie's gane tae Melville Castle
Boots and spurs on' a
Tae bid the ladies a' fareweel
Before he gaed awa'.
Willie's young and blythe and bonny
Lo'd by yen an a',
O whit will all the lasses dae
When Willie gaes awa'.

The first he met was Lady Kate,
She led him thru' the ha'
An' wi' a sad and sorry hert
She let the teardrop fa'.
Beside the fire sted Lady Grace
Said nay a werd of a',
She thocht that she was share o' him
Before he gaed awa'.

Then ben the house came Lady Bell,
'Good thra ye need not craw,
Mebe the lad will fancy me
An' disappoint ye a''.
Down the stairs tripped Lady Jean
The floor among them a',
'Oh lasses trust in providence
An' ye'll get husband a''.

As on his horse he rade awa'
They gathered roun' the door,
He gaily waved his bonnet blue
They set up sic a roar.
Their cries their tears brought Willie
    back
He kissed them yen an' a':
'O lasses bide 'til I come home
An' then – I'll wed ye a''.

DAYBREAK

Stephen Spender

At dawn she lay with her profile at that angle
Which, when she sleeps, seems the carved face of an angel.
Her hair a harp, the hand of a breeze follows
And plays, against the white cloud of the pillows
Then, in a flush of rose, she woke, and her eyes that opened
Swam in blue through her rose flesh that dawned.
'My dream becomes my dream,' she said, 'come true.
I waken from you to my dream of you.'
Oh, my own wakened dream then dared assume
The audacity of her sleep. Our dreams
Poured into each other's arms, like streams.

TAM I' THE KIRK

Violet Jacob

O Jean, my Jean, when the bell ca's the congregation
Ower valley and hill wi' the ding frae its iron mou',
When a'body's thoughts is set on their ain salvation,
Mine's set on you.

There's a reid rose lies in the Buik o' the Word afore ye
That was growin' braw on the bush at the keek o' day,
But the lad that pu'd yon flower i' the mornin's glory
He canna pray.

He canna pray; but there's none i' the kirk will heed him
Whaur he sits sae still his lane at the side o' the wa',
For nane but the reid rose kens what my lassie gied him,
It and us twa.

He canna sing for the sang that his ain he'rt raises;
He canna see for the mist that's afore his een,
And a voice droons the hale of the psalms and the paraphrases
Crying 'Jean! Jean! Jean!'

THE LOST WORLD OF THE KALAHARI

Laurens van der Post

Here at the sip-wells we found that the Bushman made also a special bow, a 'love-bow', as much an instrument of love between men and women as Cupid's bow was in the affairs of gods and ancient heroes. A Bushman, in love, carved a tiny little bow and arrow out of a sliver of the bone of a gemsbok, a great and noble animal with a lovely sweep of long crescent horn on its proud head. The bow was most beautifully made, about three inches long and matched with tiny arrows made out of stems of a sturdy grass that grew near water. The minute quiver was made from the quill of a giant bustard, the largest flying bird in the desert. The Bushman would stain the head of his arrows with a special potion and set out to stalk the lady of his choice. When he had done this successfully he would then shoot an arrow into her rump. If, on impact, she pulled out and destroyed the arrow, it was a sign that his courtship had failed. If she kept it intact then it was proof that he had succeeded.

A RING PRESENTED TO JULIA

Robert Herrick

Julia, I bring
To thee this ring,
Made for thy finger fit;
To show by this,
That our love is
(Or should be) like to it.

Close though it be,
The joint is free:
So when Love's yoke is on,
It must not gall,
Or fret at all
With hard oppression.

But it must play
Still either way;
And be, too, such a yoke,

As not too wide,
To over-slide;
Or be so strait to choke.

So, we who bear,
This beam, must rear
Ourselves to such a height:
As that the stay
Of either may
Create the burden light.

And as this round
Is no where found
To flaw, or else to sever:
So let our love
As endless prove;
And pure as Gold for ever.

THE ORDEAL OF RICHARD FEVEREL

George Meredith

He drew close to her to read the nearest features of the vision. She could no more laugh off the piercing fervour of his eyes. Her volubility fluttered under his deeply wistful look, and now neither voice was high and they were mutually constrained.

'You see,' she murmured, 'we are old acquaintances.'

Richard, with his eyes still intently fixed on her, returned: 'You are very beautiful!'

The words slipped out. Perfect simplicity is unconsciously audacious. Her overpowering beauty struck his heart, and, like an instrument that is touched and answers to the touch, he spoke.

Miss Desborough made an effort to trifle with this terrible directness; but his eyes would not be gainsaid, and checked her lips. She turned away from them, her bosom a little rebellious. Praise so passionately spoken, and by one who has been a damsel's first dream, dreamed of nightly many long nights, and clothed in the virgin silver of her thoughts in bud, praise from him is coin the heart cannot reject, if it would. She quickened her steps.

'I have offended you!' said a mortally wounded voice across her shoulder.

That he should think so were too dreadful.

'Oh, no, no! you would never offend me.' She gave him her whole sweet face.

'Then why – why do you leave me?'

'Because,' she hesitated, 'I must go.'

'No. You must not go. Why must you go? Do not go.'

'Indeed I must,' she said, pulling at the obnoxious broad brim of her hat; and, interpreting a pause he made for his assent to her rational resolve, shyly looking at him, she held her hand out, and said, 'Good-bye,' as if it were a natural thing to say.

The hand was pure white – white and fragrant as the frosted blossom of a May night. It was the hand whose shadow, cast before, he had last night bent his head reverentially above, and kissed – resigning himself thereupon over to execution for payment of the penalty of such daring – by such bliss well rewarded.

He took the hand, and held it, gazing between her eyes.

'Good-bye,' she said again, as frankly as she could, and at the same time slightly compressing her fingers on his in token of adieu. It was a signal for his to close firmly upon hers.

'You will not go?'

'Pray, let me,' she pleaded, her sweet brows suing in wrinkles.

'You will not go?' Mechanically he drew the white hand nearer his thumping heart.

'I must,' she faltered piteously.

'You will not go?'

'Oh, yes! yes!'

'Tell me. Do you wish to go?'

The question was a subtle one. A moment or two she did not answer, and then forswore herself, and said, 'Yes.'

'Do you – you wish to go?' He looked with quivering eyelids under hers.

A fainter 'Yes' responded.

'You wish – wish to leave me?' His breath went with the words.

'Indeed I must.'

Her hand became a closer prisoner.

All at once an alarming delicious shudder went through her frame. From him to her it coursed, and back from her to him. Forward and back love's electric messenger rushed from heart to heart, knocking at each, till it surged tumultuously against the bars of its prison, crying out for its mate. They stood trembling in unison, a lovely couple under these fair heavens of the morning.

When he could get his voice it said: 'Will you go?'

But she had none to reply with, and could only mutely bend upward her gentle wrist.

'Then, farewell!' he said, and, dropping his lips to the soft fair hand, kissed it, and hung his head, swinging away from her, ready for death.

Strange, that now she was released she should linger by him. Strange, that his audacity, instead of the executioner, brought blushes and timid tenderness to his side, and the sweet words: 'You are not angry with me?'

'With you, O beloved!' cried his soul. 'And you forgive me, fair charity!'

'I think it was rude of me to go without thanking you again,' she said, and again proffered her hand.

The sweet heaven-bird shivered out his song above him. The gracious glory of heaven fell upon his soul. He touched her hand, not moving his eyes from her, nor speaking, and she, with a soft word of farewell, passed across the stile, and up the pathway through the dewy shades of the copse, and out of the arch of the light, away from his eyes.

SONNETS FROM THE PORTUGUESE
Elizabeth Barrett Browning

How do I love thee? Let me count the ways.
I love thee to the depth and breadth and height
My soul can reach, when feeling out of sight
For the ends of Being and ideal Grace.
I love thee to the level of everyday's
Most quiet need, by sun and candle-light.
I love thee freely, as men strive for Right;
I love thee purely, as they turn from Praise.
I love thee with the passion put to use
In my old griefs, and with my childhood's faith.
I love thee with a love I seemed to lose
With my lost saints - I love thee with the breath,
Smiles, tears, of all my life! - and, if God choose,
I shall but love thee better after death.

THE GREEN STICK

Malcolm Muggeridge

Montreux Station in the very early morning waiting for Kitty seemed about as far away from the USSR and Oumansky, from Berlin and the storm-troopers out in the streets, as it was possible to be. The coffee so hot and fragrant, the rolls so crisp, the butter so creamy; the waiter so obliging, his hair so sleek and black, his face so sallow, his coat so fresh and spotlessly white. Everything and everyone so solid and so durable. Even Kitty's train, roaring in exactly on time, was part of the omnipresent orderliness. There is always a dread on such occasions that somehow the rendezvous will not be kept; that arrangements which seemed so precise will somehow have gone awry. So one studies the gathering faces with mounting anxiety; every sort of face showing up except the particular one in question, until, at last, there it is; unmistakable, unique, infinitely dear. Waving to Kitty in the distance when I see her, holding one son's hand and another son in her arms, a Shakespearean tag comes into my mind: 'Hang there like fruit, my soul, till the tree die.' What is love but a face, instantly recognisable in a sea of faces? A spotlight rather than a panning shot? This in contradistinction to power, which is a matter of numbers, of crowd scenes. I heard of an inscription on a stone set up in North Africa which reads: 'I, the captain of a Legion of Rome, have learnt and pondered this truth, that there are in life but two things, love and power, and no man can have both.' Some twenty centuries later, I append my own amen.

YOU ARE THE NEW DAY

John David

I will love you more than me
And more than yesterday,
If you can but prove to me
You are the new day.
Send the sun in time for dawn,
Let the birds all hail the morning;
Love of life will urge me say,
You are the new day.

When I lay me down at night,
Knowing we must pay,
Thoughts occur that night
Might stay yesterday.
Thoughts that we as humans small,
Could slow worlds and end it all,
Lie around me where they fall
Before the new day.

One more day when time
Is running out for everyone.
Like a breath I knew would come
I reach for the new day.
Hope is my philosophy,
Just needs days in which to be,
Love of life is hope for me
Born on a new day.

You are the new day.

LOVE'S PHILOSOPHY

Percy Bysshe Shelley

The fountains mingle with the river
And the rivers with the Ocean.
The winds of Heaven mix for ever
With a sweet emotion;
Nothing in the world is single;
All things by a law divine
In one spirit meet and mingle
Why not I with thine? –

See the mountains kiss high Heaven
And the waves clasp one another;
No sister-flower would be forgiven
If it disdained its brother;
And the sunlight clasps the earth
And the moonbeams kiss the sea:
What is all this sweet work worth
If thou kiss not me?

NATURE, MAN AND WOMAN
Alan W. Watts

It is commonly thought that, of all people, lovers behold one another in the most unrealistic light, and that in their encounter is but the mutual projection of extravagant ideals. But may it not be that nature has allowed them to see for the first time what a human being is, and that the subsequent disillusion is not the fading of dream into reality but the strangling of reality with an all too eager embrace?

THRICE TOSSE THESE OAKEN ASHES
Thomas Campion

Thrice tosse these oaken ashes in the
    ayre,
Thrice sit thou mute in this inchanted
    chayre,
And thrice-three times tye up this true
    love's knot,
And murmer soft 'shee will, or shee will
    not.'

Goe, burn these poys'nous weedes in
    yon blew fire,
These screech-owles fethers, and this
    prickling bryer,
This cypresse gathered at a dead man's
    grave;
That all my feares and cares an end may
    have.

Then come you Fayries! dance with me
    a round!
Melt her hard hart with your melodious
    sound!
In vaine are all the charms I can devise:
She hath an arte to breake them with
    her eyes.

TREATISE ON SPIRITUAL FRIENDSHIP
Aelred of Rievaulx

In a kiss, two spirits meet, mingle, and become one; and as a result there arises in the mind a wonderful feeling of delight that awakens and binds together the love of them that kiss.

THE RIDDLE SONG

Anon

I gave my love a cherry without a stone,
I gave my love a chicken without a bone,
I gave my love a story without an end,
I gave my love a baby with no cryin'.

How can there be a cherry without a
    stone,
How can there be a chicken without a
    bone,
How can there be a story without an
    end,
How can there be a baby with no cryin'.

A cherry when it's blooming it has no
    stone,
A chicken when it's pippin' it has no
    bone,
And the story that I love you it has no
    end,
And a baby when it's sleeping has no
    cryin'.

BUT ROSES FADE

Sappho

But roses fade, and summer's sun will
    end,
    And oaths be broken.
So never swear to Love. Or if you do
Remember oaths can make no rose
    eternal,
Nor keep the sun from setting, nor
    bestow
    A second summer.

JULIET

Hilaire Belloc

How did the party go in Portman
    Square?
I cannot tell you; Juliet was not there.

And how did Lady Gaster's party go?
Juliet was next me and I do not know.

LOVING

Noël Coward

Loving is more important than being *in* love.
If one can grow from the other you're all right;
sometimes it does, sometimes it doesn't,
but when it does you're in for a long run.

Love
and
Richard

Love and Richard

31 January 1956

... Mary, I study to love you better and better, to love what is truly you, to love what is best in you because that increases my respect and admiration for you and to love what is at fault in you because in that, too, I know you – and knowing and loving you is what I desire and need to do more than anything else in the world.

– Richard

The above extract is from a letter to me by Richard Selig during the period leading up to our engagement and eventual marriage. Even when I was being taken to task, the letters were couched in the language of love.

All true poets exclude nothing from enquiry and perhaps that is why everything in life held a fascination for Richard Selig. Nothing was too insignificant or dull for his scrutiny. (Walking along the street one day in New York he told me excitedly that he was planning to write an essay on car registration numbers!) His sense of wonder remained unimpaired to the end. Though he was acutely aware that man's life on earth, especially his own as it turned out, is brief, he did not for that reason cut short his search for meaning.

At university he studied, among other things, psychology and comparative religion, and though he had no religious upbringing at home, he was very conscious of the spiritual dimension. He was not a Christian in the sense of being baptised into the Church. Indeed those who knew him would never have considered him in any way religious. But in fact he was a very God-orientated person. He was fascinated by Christ – strangely, I thought at first. He understood much more about my Catholic faith than I, a cradle Catholic, did.

He lived a richly varied and full life. 'He fell on books,' wrote Peter Levi, 'as he did on life with a violent and exigent hunger.' Thinker, searcher, seeker: a singularly aware individual, his insights into the mystery and nature of love were remarkable in one so young (he died at the age of twenty-seven). Some of those insights he has shared with us through his writings. He conveyed to me his conviction that mystery is as much an essential part of art and of the work of the artist as it is of religion. It has to do with the *Spirit,* in other words with God. God and his mysterious ways exercised both his heart and his mind.

'From the words of the poet,' wrote Tagore, 'men take what meanings please them; yet their last meaning points to thee.' For me much of Richard Selig's poetry points to the Almighty. A book of selected poems published in 1962 is now out of print and other poems have appeared from time to time in various magazines, but for this chapter I have chosen some of my own favourites from among his published and unpublished works.

THE ISLAND: NOVEMBER 1953

Who dwells here dwells in the wind. Only the flesh is past,
Concealed under dirt are its inexplicable ways;
Only the sigh remains, only the unbidden stays,
Only the rocks contain, the sun heaps up the last
Injunctions to the conscious animal that rest
Is the grail of all its agony, that death is the happiest
Welcomer, the surest healer for the sickened brain;
For this ungainly beast hopes heartily but dies in pain:
Because its flesh is mutinous, its thought runs wild,
Its gnarled tendons snap like twigs and the mild-
Mannered worms lunch on its rageless spleen.
Who dwells here dwells in the wind. The wordless sigh
Is what's left, and beaches, ruins, greenery,
Some scuttling foragers, tame and indifferent scenery,
An island bleak and no home to this poetry.
Let strange guests depart from the stranger dead;
Let them sail away as they came, still uninstructed
By the elusive agony which drove them to islands;
Let them go as they came, unanswered and in silence;
This is no place for the living, where the wind sighs
In endless dalliance with speech but never speaks,
For the word stops at the roots of grass, leaks
Into the maggots' mouths, slides humming, slips and cries
Who breathes this air warms no angel in the lungs,
Wind comes no nearer to spirit than trees
To heaven, nor comes flesh nearer to love than seas
Do to the moon: angels and things speak in alien tongues.

I come to this island, Circe, to be changed by thee
Into another animal: this trip is too long.
Troy was a great city; I wrought her great wrong:
Her men were as good and handsome as we,
But they were men, and more dangerous than brutes.
Their strange language, the harsh notes of their flutes
Enraged us: yet dying for them seemed no different.
The crash as they fell, the alizarin blood, the groan:
These seemed the same. And suddenly reverent,
We gathered the limp slain like lovers left too soon alone
And put them in fresh graves as if to sleep:
So change me, Circe, for as a man my image makes me weep.

MY FRIENDS: A FABLE

One day when I hadn't been eating anything, because I was ill with fever, Unicorn came in to see Swan. I saw him from my bedroom window, but I didn't say anything.

Unicorn came in through a hole in the back fence. He wasn't very big. He was shy, though, and I could see that Swan was having a hard time with him. She kept to the middle of the pond, her head down facing him. She managed to look very cross with Unicorn, and Unicorn hung his head shamefully. Swan kept saying things I couldn't hear, and Unicorn nodded and wept. Then Swan became more gentle. She went nearer to Unicorn. She waddled out of the pond to stand beside him. Unicorn sat with his forelegs out and hindlegs folded under him, but only for a little while. Soon he was up: 'Goodbye, Swan,' I heard him say.

'Goodbye, Lord,' Swan said.

The next day I wasn't ill any more. I went out to talk with Swan.

'Swan! Swan! Who is Unicorn?'

Swan went slowly around and around the pond saying nothing.

'Please tell me, Swan. He's such a charming fellow, and I would like him to come again.'

Swan nodded her head slowly up and down.

'You called him "Lord", Swan. Is he a grand person? He's rather small and delicate. I . . .'

'You talk too much!' Swan said.

'You're not very polite, Swan. You don't answer any questions. I have to ask and ask for hours sometimes before you say anything at all.'

'And you don't *think* before you ask your questions!' Swan replied.

'Please don't be angry, Swan.'

'I'm sorry, Man,' Swan said. 'Unicorn is very royal, and some of your kind were hunting him when he took refuge in your backyard. He said that he wanted them to find him, but that he was afraid. You see, they have been chasing him so long they are angry. They sought him for love in the beginning. I told him not to let himself get caught.'

WHY THE MINNOWS' FLASH

Why the minnows' flash or last night's
   moon
Should so deflect my thought, I cannot
   say:
Because your tears this morning fell so
   soon
To humble me, I fear they marred the
   day.

THE ELEMENTS

The brain is crowded with its own past substance. Perhaps it is the house of the soul and perhaps not. For the soul travels and is never at home. If my finger hurts it is because the soul wishes to eject an unnecessary distraction. She centres there and pushes. Her effort causes my pain. For pain is the encounter of the less dense with the more dense. A rock encounters my finger, the finger encounters the soul and I feel pain. What is the soul's occupation? She is busy avoiding encounters. Being the least dense of all things, including light, she is the most susceptible to pain. For the desire of everything is to sustain its qualities. And pain obstructs the completion of that desire. Pain alters the identity of everything. That which is most dense occupies the least space; that which is least dense may occupy all space. I say 'may' because the soul, for example, attempting to fill its rightful domain, often encounters usurpers. But the soul is relentless and, though it is the most susceptible to, is the least alterable by pain.

The most durable of substances – rock – for example, is slowly hewn and sundered of its nature by the subtle processes of wind and water; and may even be boiled by the igneous invader. Metal corrodes by exposure to oxygen; its envy compels it to combine with the freer element. The ignorant waters, seduced by the liberties of warm air, sublime into a vapour and ascend. But like the best of lovers air blows warm and cold, and the sad waters will not be had again and so they freeze. But what of air? Is he not victimised also? Is he inaccessible to pain? No. Light is less than he. Light comes invisibly across vast emperies of space from the bubbling sun to make the wind and the day. Air refracts and forms a whole society of currents to elude the ravishment of light. But to no avail. And having no recourse, vengeful and desperate, he seeks to occupy another's place: he hacks at the ocean, saws at mountains and bridges, and moaning topples the great trees.

THE PRAIRIE

In that strange return when even the leaves were angry,
Small birds broke from the boughs in savage singing.
It was late May: drought champed the new stalks,
The sun shingled the pale earth, the wind coughed.
My sweat was all the juice from east to west
That freely flowed, my veins the fullest river,
My skull the coolest cave. Winter wheat lay stacked,
The buzzards wheeled, the lean jack rabbit jumped
And lizards licked their supper from the air.

How can I tell you, stranger? Is drought more harsh,
Prairie more desolate, because some painted men
Whom space and pride had taught that beasts were spirits
Wandered here and fought unequal skirmishes
Against strange weapons and a stranger greed that could not stop?

LAMENT OF MY MOTHER

Spring is here, my mate is gone,
The earth is richer with him I loved:
No reason nor eternal stone
Could mark this loss, this loneliness;
Whatever shared, what held, what
    thrived
In us, no time nor death could sever.
But the shadow of awakening boughs
On the awakened ground, spring's
    comeliness
Like his each morning stirred from
    drowze
And the nights of our long love's fever
Bring to mind and bring no more
    forever
My mate who is gone when Spring is
    over.

HOROSCOPE

When, at such hour that we meet to change our myth,
Assure and calculate our dreams with money,
Merger fates, then troop from the darkened cafe:
You whom now I do not know shall be
My great, predominating Venus;
I, your Mars. Our influential way –
Half war and half in love – shall change, and change.

For lo! on starless and on starry streets
We shall elude the navigator's fix and count.
With new, with unknown numbers suddenly appear
(And run to north and south) the avenues
With future names. We, each other following
Through all the other fables fixed for ever,
Believe our own more free.
But dawn reveals
The crystalline Apollo; night brings dim Phoebe,
Orion's bands, Libra's blindfold, Cancer's
Claw, and Scorpion's eternal poison.

A SONG OF TREES

All summer long I steeped in sunlight,
    Stored up abundant heat;
Not one tree but a forest was I,
O gladly green beneath the sky.
    All wing'd and furry things
        Played house with me;
With O their flashing wings,
Their gentle industry,
In nest, or hive, or burrow
    - O Pity, have pity
On small things: they built not knowing
    sorrow.

O Lord, I stand, a patient host,
    To winter's wind opposed,
    And firm in Thy firm Will,
        I shall not kneel.
But see! The little lives are lost
    That hoped and thrived in me
        Who seemed their friend
        And proved their gallows
    In Nature's treachery.
My roots cry out to make an end:
Lord, I would no more defend,
And then betray, unless Thy Mercy
    follows.

THE UNICORN

For two years the Commission for the Collection of Horns had been preparing an expedition. The members were chosen for five qualities or attainments: masculinity, physical fitness, intelligence, youth, experience as hunters, and vision. Most of the applicants fulfilled the first four with ease, but were disqualified for want of the fifth. Vision, according to the commission, consisted of skill in interpretation of dreams, of success in composing allegorical verse and in prophecy; and lacking sanctity, the members must at least have a kindly disposition towards God. Needless to say the majority of the members selected were poets, a few were priests and a very small number of others were suspected of sainthood.

On the day they set out the sun shone propitiously. Everyone was equipped with a small copy of a picture of their prey. It had been drawn for the occasion by an artist who had followed the scant and fragmentary descriptions that had trickled into the commission's archives for centuries. These descriptions were filed in the Mythical Division, under Unicorn, 'being a species of beast, only one of which is supposed to exist, with a single conical horn in the center of its brow ... and is said to be immortal'. The picture that each member bore with him was entitled 'conjectural portrait' and was of an animal with the body of a highly bred, lithe and delicate horse, the size of a large dog. Its nose was elongated, merging into a chinless, full-lipped mouth that formed a perfect semicircular, very loving and permanent smile. The eyes were large and exceedingly gentle; the nostrils round, prominent and sensitive. It was not the beast's ferocity that caused apprehension among the hunters, but rather it was the extreme rarity, not to say singularity, of the beast considered in the light of its terrifying kindliness. The hunters were all accustomed to ferocity, cunning or timidity in their prey, such as are exhibited respectively by lions, foxes and rabbits, but never had they encountered a beast whose chief natural defense was kindliness. Kindliness! How do you snare it? Indeed how do you track it? Since there was believed to be only one unicorn, the question also arose as to where to begin looking for it.

For many days and nights they traveled towards the place where the sun first shows itself and where the communities of men grow fewer and sparser, until they came to an immense and seemingly endless forest under whose aegis neither rain nor light were able to encroach. Indeed it was very dark, a darkness of green, inside there, and the hunters paused to confer amongst themselves before entering it. A discussion ensued which lasted for many hours with nothing as the upshot. Finally some went to sleep until a plan were formulated, others prayed, others prattled for days, constructing vast analogies and losing themselves in a forest of rhetoric. One of the sleepers woke, declaring that he had had a dream which concerned the Unicorn. One of those who prayed asked the dreamer to tell his dream. The dream was duly described and a groan of insight and thanksgiving escaped from the breast of the one who prayed. He enlightened the other hunters in very persuasive tones as to the import of the dream: that they should find the guidance they sought among the inhabitants of a village not far from where they were.

A deputation of volunteers set out for the village. After several hours walk they found a small collection of houses surrounded by grassy hills punctuated with sheep and rivulets. In the midst of the houses was a clearing and in the middle of the clearing was a well. At the well a girl with long hair and a long skirt down to the toes was drawing water. Beside the well an old man sat on a three-legged stool watching the approach of the strangers, nodding and smiling, his arms folded across his chest.

'Father,' said one of the hunters, 'we are looking for the beast with one horn,' and showed the old man the picture.

'Yes', said the old man, 'you have come for help and you have done wisely. My child,' he said tugging at the skirts of the girl, 'go with these men and show them the way into the forest and help them with their quest.'

She drew up the full bucket, placed it by the old man, wiping her hands on her skirt. 'Father, please take the water to the house,' and she went off with the hunters.

CANZONETTA

O in the ever dark
Pity of my lady
Song of lark
Green love is ready.

O how has she
This lovely lady
Made heart unsteady?

O spring, I sing this
Coin for a kiss,

Love has no pity, lady,

Take this.

O in the ever dark
Pity of my lady
Song of lark
Green love is ready.

A MEDITATION IN LENT

During the forty days of desert the white sun filled
And readied the spirit for the innocence that killed.
Within the simple landscape, sky and sand, he thought
About what any Jew might think: of love and death,
Of fragrant cedars long ago, of legendary faith,
And thought of Moses surely, and that promise sought
Of homeland, peace and plenitude; while flesh waned
And spirit searched the fire.
Who sinned and how atoned
The vultures could not tell; but one uneasy creature, man,
Had troubled the wide globe with thought of God and sin.

No wrong was done but it was doubled, given back
And back until exhaustion let revenging arms go slack
And peace was made synonymous with death or sleep.
Because he could not pacify the raging heart or keep
The stranger off his land, or lust within his breast;
Because the trumpet of his appetite oppressed,
And drums of fear forewarned, he took to war and flayed
His brother, stripped him of the flesh that made them kin;
But found no peace, nor pleasures taken unafraid,
Because the spoils were too rich with blood, too rich with sin.

During the forty days that wide confessional
Of sand and sky became a battleground where all
The floods and sudden terrors, years of wandering,
Began tell upon the young Jew's mind.
Beginning
with rain that fell unceasingly from heaven, then bread,
Then warriors, then blood, then lightning, plague on plague,
The dark angel stooping over all with lamb's blood sprayed
The doors of the mortal ghetto - the linked bones broke,
The temporal chain unraveled, the mind unspun its truth
And he found courage during forty days to death.

The white-hot sun bloomed within his mind;
The desert scorched and healed the lank flesh;
The spirit entered at all doors, awake and fresh;
The rivers of his blood were ready to unwind.
During the forty days man's grossest wish
Came true: a perfect lamb, a perfect naked man
To torment and then kill, and plant his death within
The relics of all thirsty love, a youthful God who can
Take on the burden of our death and live again;
While we, bearing and burying, sip the wine of his veins.

THE POLESTAR

Here, no foothold is sure. Like huge
  water
The night sky flows overhead. The stars
  flicker.
The source of their faint radiance stands
  above them.
In that country the land is firm, the light
  is constant.

Orion hangs head down. The Dog Star's
  glazed look
Crosses heaven like a rabid beacon. The
  stiff Crab floats by.
I look for Polaris: and there, rounding
  its tiny circle,
My lodestar spins. All is flung in pieces,
  far flung.

Beneath me the cooling star-fragment I
  stand on
Prepares upheavals that will smash the
  man-fashioned stones
I prize the most, and cast the bones that
  upheld the men
I most admire into lava or the depths of a
  new sea.

ENTRANCE OF
THE GLADIATORS

In a minute I'm going out there. It is time
now to think. There won't be any time
later. And at least this is my own part of
ritual. When my thinking ends they take
over: the emperor and his girl friends and
thousands of Romans.

I think of my friends – the only friends I
have ever had – the friends whom I have
killed in this arena. It is all in this, something they cannot know: to kill a man as I
do I must first make his acquaintance,
find how to love him and then kill him. It
can be done no other way. We are after
all only human.

It is time. His name is Canabillus, a tall
man from the northern provinces. I have
never met him. He comes towards me.
They expect a real fight.

I can see his eyes now. They are blue.
He has not waited. He looks at me
lovingly. I have saluted.

WORSHIP

Solemn as trees priests in their pale
  robes
Transfigure the air, engraft the sight
With fruit-heavy, death to the bearer,
  ribs
Of branches, watery fingers, words.

People rooted to floors and walls falter
Like ferns, all motion at the top,
At bottom decay, for God cannot stop
To pluck them out: stars float on the
  altar.

Solemn as trees monks in their dark
  robes
Deliver the stain of things to itches and
  rubs;
For weary is their way, weary by prayer,
        Worn
More holy by the world's failure to be
  born.
Because the long womb is stuffed by
  chance
Because stars glisten on the heads of
  saints,
        leaves dance.

TWO UNDERWORLDS

In the garden of Persephone trees grow in the dark.
  A strong wind blows when trains come.

In Hades there are four rivers, and there are the dead.
  It is never cold. You never see birds.

Odysseus, Aeneas, Orpheus went there and escaped alive.
  You rarely see three-headed dogs on week-days.

To get there one crosses the Styx by ferry. Charon is the ferryman's name.
  When you get on, one man closes all the doors.

The architecture of Hades is either Classical, Gothic or Baroque.
  Among the white tiles there are signs telling you where you are.
Poets find Hades an evocative image, being the kingdom of death.
  It is best to concentrate on one's newspaper.

The Christian counterpart of Hades is the Inferno.
  People seldom excuse themselves when they push you.

Jesus Christ harrowed the place, leading the good people to paradise.
  Between stations the tunnel is dark. It is too noisy to sing.

ELEGY FOR MY UNCLE

Tell me that sorrow is not grand,
Earth cannot contain his quiet,
That I remember him and understand
Death's coming; love him and deny it.

Rather I shall know him here
In the monument of blood, in a soft
    hand
Gathering my flesh; and fear
Or love his ghost as a child of my mind.

How shall I consecrate this time
To the meaning of death in season:
Summer again, but am I not the same
Who loved him for a child's reason?

What does death mean, more than his
    life,
More than I remember or can say,
More than June, his brothers in their
    graves,
Uncles all and bones of my blood put
    away?

Who shall I say has died; who believes
That death means anything at all to
    anyone:
Harry was dying, and now earth receives
What no one wants ... his life, this poem,
    undone.

SONG FOR A TEMPEST

That we may learn the spirit's dance,
Be permanent as bone,
We must become love's flagellants
And never lie alone;
For sanctity is founded on
Relics of flesh and bone.
Go forth as Ariel went
Freely to enjoy your element

For love a man has built a city,
Another burnt it down;
Some men lived in piety,
Some killed for bread or crown:
All such human vanity
Love has overthrown.
Go forth as Ariel went
Freely to enjoy your element

Each lover in his time has learned
The history of sighs,
Why Ilium's towers were burned,
Why every infant cries;
For travail of the flesh has earned
More flesh than paradise.
Go forth as Ariel went
Freely to enjoy your element

Prospero has drowned his book,
The actors all are glad:
Justice done to all alike;
The magic used was good.
Sigh and take another look
At how the world is made;
Go forth as Ariel went
Freely to enjoy your element

And when the bones can no more stand,
When pleasure has no house,
Because the flesh lies limp and blind,
And love has been let loose,
Learn what breaks the spirit's bond,
Why love is made to lose;
Go forth as Ariel went
Freely to enjoy your element

TENEBRAE

The gorgeous beast he was as man
As ghost he was no less because
The whisper of the wings began
To stir the loins and break the laws

That made him stranger to his
    creatures.
And in her womb he perched: the price
He paid for love was human nature.
Friday's payment, Sunday's paradise.

And then he rose, a winged ghost;
Flew from pain in the world's eyes
But left his love, though life lost.
Friday's payment, Sunday's paradise.

The priest's eyes pierce the cloud
Of incense, mumbled liturgies,
And see his Lord in a torn shroud.
Friday's payment, Sunday's paradise.

One by one the lights go out,
One by one like time that dies.
He dies in darkness with a shout:
Friday's payment, Sunday's paradise.

THE FOUNTAIN
To T.S.E.

He walks in the valley, through still glades, by streams,
Up hill to the sunny level, or down to the shore.
He can imagine Paradise and can describe to you
Blade by blade, flower by flower, its lovely slopes;
But wherever he inhabits nothing survives for long.
His breath soughs mortality across the land.
As far as he can see the green leaf turns brown.

He worships the naked lineaments of sunlight
As if the sun itself substantiates his own mind,
The bare sun burning the senses like grass.
Nature he despises. Her multiplicity,
Her changes, her alien presence in his blood
Obscure the single radiance he seeks: naked Truth,
Cruel Beauty - flames without bodies - parch his mind.

The arid landscape he chooses to inhabit fits
The sapless mind that animates him. Like a desolate fountain
(A marble Psyche rising from its center) that pours
No longer, his mind still holds the shape of Beauty
Yet he cannot reproduce it, nor will his fancy take
Impression from it. Nothing will eject the dry
Perfection in his mind, but the cold night will shatter it.

WHERE BUBBLES DAWDLE

Where bubbles dawdle, green wands wave and tadpoles jerk;
Where slow pond water slowly scurling flows,
Seeming still - the sky and half the meadow mirrored;
And moderate Nature rests in pondside reeds,
Drowses in the meadow, dreams in water volumes:
Everywhere one looks, tranquillity does soothe the gaze,
Peace placates the wild senses, and truth lies sleeping.
Look down into the pond, change your element.
Let Fancy take you. Plunge down. Your ear cannot hear,
Your lungs dare not stir. Yet the blood buzzes:
Fancy feeds you air. Your eyes are clear.
You swim among silence in the green world.

(Beginnings of a long poem unwritten. This was the last thing he wrote.)

THE PHOENIX

As great as earth with child or sun with fire, the dawn
Of his life breaks. Annunciation cancels the cold
Nest of ashes where he lies dead. Now the winged spawn
Of love's hot mystery grows young while we grow old.
If sudden or slow agony, if sleep or pain
Find out the fire, choke the source and drown the man
Then in that limp shell may be the busy princes reign,
May the bee suck and the slow sun kindle another man.
In the heart's red image of feast and flame
The cool, arterial wine rots in the house of his name.

As busily as stars gnawing the hot heart of heaven
He pecks his grave, greedy again to be born.
Cold ashes that were his death are now his leaven
Raising the flesh once more to bleed upon a thorn
And share his limbs into the infinite mouth
Of human kind to feed the hunger of that fire
Where spirit melts and merges into the hazardous truth
And man and God burn with one desire.
Love's gain and loss, the heavy claims of earth,
The mortgage of all living kind cannot escape his birth.

With one desire heart breaks and angels fall,
God dies and man corrupts: who knows the remedy?
The stars recede, the elements increase, and small
And weak as grass we and our citadels decay.
As we prosper something dies without a cry,
A child that chokes in the womb; unseen calamities
That haunt the docks and derricks, the rich quay,
The markets, factories, all monuments of avarice.
Trading among the continents the cunning Ulysses
Grows rich while elsewhere he, the willing soldier, dies.

Ambiguous the dead to live again, the living to live
On dying: who can puzzle it? And yet our lips
Without horror his flesh and blood gladly receive.
Bearing him to distant war go the grey ships.
Money like rain slakes the parched roots of the state
And metal magnifies the glory of man's fear and greed.
Who rises from the city planted with our hate?
Who rises from the ashes, who on ashes feed?
Who dares to venture in the mortal flame
And bear once more the torture of man's name?

ELEGY FOR A DEAD CLOWN

A Prince on Saturdays with candy wealth,
I left the soiling cares of nine years old
And injured – never permanently – my health
With too much popcorn, thoughts – for nine – too old,
And prodigal laughter. My Palace (it was called)
Of Oriental charms and pleasing twilight,
Was populous with fountains, footmen, gold,
All genuine and Byzantine delight,
With ceiling starred and domed to simulate the night.

Night prepared, Night was the imperial theme
Of all this glory; where ten-cent royalty
Foregathered in the dark to share a dream,
And legiance give, in glad complicity,
To common, and unreal humanity.
I sat till nothing but the EXIT shone,
And mortal shadow swayed down shafts of light;
Till night with laughter soon had overflown
To flood that funny world, flashing black and white.

To us, who were not royal, he was King;
To him, that we were, what we are, was art,
In all his gestures there was no new thing;
We saw and recognized, we knew our part;
We said: be funny, and he broke his heart.
If humor was to love him with a custard pie,
The pie was thrown. But sometimes humor hanged,
The sweet meringue turned bitter, seemed to fly
Into the face of all that's human and can be wronged.

The youthful critic learned to punctuate
All strange and grown-up passion with his feet
(Pity for those giants would come late)
Scuffling, writhing, sighing in his seat
– Till Love – stuff ended – munched his sweet,
He only liked the things he understood:
Bank robbery, a chase, embarrassed poverty,
The cops with funny hats, the victim Good.
Precocious anger gave him taste for anarchy.

THE TIGER

By instinct cloistered and by sense
  confined,
By flesh mortgaged and by need struck
  blind,
The pining animal makes way for more:
Progenitor and victim of his kind.

Through love; and through that self-
  same mystery
Protects, instructs the tender enemy
To watch his ebb translated into youth
In love and rage that only death sets
  free.

Like the womb from which the Maker
  made
The world; like the first dawn that once
  laid
Bare impossible wonders; like the
  nothing
Whence he came, pristine and unafraid,

Emptied of the toxin of mortality,
A tranquil part of all that he could see,
The tiger stood, gazing at the sun,
At the lean, sere earth, his spirit once
  more free.

The tigress leaned her length along
  green boughs,
Crouched and crept under the fronds of
  shadows.
Her lithe lankness and her perfumed
  breath
Made drunk the air and caused the
  breeze to drowze.

She lay in wait until the tiger found
Her dreaming ambush, till they together
  crowned
The plenty of that place by gentle
  combat –
Each other's limbs in ardent armor
  bound.

Their eyes grew dim beneath the strokes
  of war;
Blood locked within their brows but not
  for anger.
Heat, touch and smell controlled their
  skirmish –
In mutual darkness, neither vanquisher.

THE COAST

As reeds or branches shake, the flushed hare leaps,
And bodies sway to tunes, to wind, to fears unseen;
As all of nature like a half-broken bell
Dins or chimes, sometimes harsh and sometimes sweet,
Its threat and melody always there, soothing or crushing;
As even the tenderest leaf holds on tenacious, faith
Bred in its green veins; or the lion, not loud enough
To outroar the storm, roars his heart out till the tackle
And scaffold of his sinew lies fallen and torn;
As hero and saint in the legend confront strange fate,
Deity claiming their lives, earth getting their bones;
As mist climbs down from the mountains and lovers complain;
As the sun and moon must navigate always over
The same track and always through changing hazard of cloud
Because, capricious and steady, the world renews itself
Under heaven: you, accepting this and perhaps, too,
My love, because you are even younger than myself
And telling you I may believe it, must learn faith
In human things, admire nature when you can,
Protest when you must, live in this mortal house
A kind witness even to the throngs of maimed that pass
Your door, live as little by fear as you can,
Believing that there are such people living that make
It worthy to be their neighbours in danger or joy,
That the one riddle, the one great enterprise,
In this world is to learn how to love and keep loving.

ON READING *SCOTT'S LAST EXPEDITION*

The hazardous career meets death
    halfway;
Who chooses active dying must endure
The thought of death much longer, see
    it lure
Him past all hope and one by one betray
His chances until mercy is a brief delay
Before the ice immures the blood; make
    sure
They know ill-luck, not fear, was cause of
    failure;
And silent, then, explore the last white
    day.

VALEDICTORY POEM

for Mr C. S. Lewis

Now you go to England's other Eye
Take with you, Sir, your pupils' love,
May th'other college of the tearful Mary
Be twin, in youth's love, to this you leave
Whose eye you opened year by year to
    see:
The Past can change but changeless is
    its glory.
    The hour when you departure take
    Let Oxford weep and Cambridge
    wake.

IN THE FABLED KINGDOM

In the fabled kingdom of my heart
The Hawk pursues his love,
Breaks from the sky with talons hooked
To claim the tender dove.

No hawk knows better grace
Nor dove a deeper pain
Than I, alone in this dark place
Loved by beasts of the brain.

Love
and
Separation

Love and Separation

Parting is bitter and weeping vain,
And all true lovers will meet again,
And no fate can sever my love from me,
For his heart is the river and mine the sea.

This quotation from an Irish song 'The Parting' is an example of one of the perennial themes of love poetry. There is indeed a sense in which neither time nor space can separate lovers, as illustrated in the intensely poignant case of the medieval couple Abelard and Heloise:

> For Heloise, Abelard and her life as a religious were inseparably linked. She had become a nun, not to thrust human love into the past, but to prove its reality in the present. The present had not taken the place of the past. Nor had the cloister become for her a substitute for Abelard. In the one person, there is Heloise the nun and Heloise the wife of Abelard ... Each had been necessary to the other – to the welfare, the comfort, the redemption of the other. They can no more be separated than in a melody can treble from bass, bass from treble (*Heloise,* Elizabeth Hamilton).

In many circumstances the very presence of love makes pain inevitable. Separation in small doses is not necessarily a bad thing; it prevents relationships from stagnating, it avoids that corrosive taking of each other for granted that can be so destructive of love. Separation judiciously rationed can make lovers see each other with fresh eyes and the pain of such separations can purify and ennoble a love. The great wish of true love is to be with the beloved for ever and any obstacle to that possibility can be painful. Death which is the final separation is like losing part of oneself, but even that is potentially fruitful as Anthony Padovano points out: 'more impressive than the brokenness of our hearts is the fact that we have a heart and that it is tender enough to suffer. Even a scar tells us of more than the wound we have sustained: it tells us that we have prevailed.'

The experience of separation through death, as I know, is devastating, but like all suffering it can be unexpectedly enlightening. Death, that great winnower, jolts life into perspective. Few things concentrate the mind more quickly so that we can see clearly the difference between the wheat and the chaff. We have been made to know the briefness of life so as to gain wisdom of heart. Perhaps that is what Nietzsche meant when he said that the growth of wisdom could be judged accurately by the decline of ill-temper.

We spend our lives building up a web of relationships and dependencies which become woven into the fabric of our lives. We are contingent beings not only in relation to the Creator but also to one another. As John Donne so nicely puts it:

> No man is an island, entire of itself; every man is a piece of the continent, a part of the main; any man's death diminishes me, because I am involved in Mankind; And therefore never send to know for whom the bell tolls; It tolls for thee.

To the believer, of course, death itself is not the end, but more like a horizon, a limit to what one can see. For the Christian there is no permanent separation.

ONE HARD LOOK

Robert Graves

Small gnats that fly
In hot July
And lodge in sleeping ears
Can rouse therein
A trumpet's din
With Day of Judgement fears.

Small mice at night
Can wake more fright
Than lions at midday;
A straw will crack
The camel's back -
There is no easier way.

One smile relieves
A heart that grieves
Though deadly sad it be,
And one hard look
Can close the book
That lovers love to see.

O WALY, WALY

Anon

The water is wide I cannot get o'er,
    and neither have I wings to fly.
Give me a boat that will carry two,
    and both shall row, my love and I.
O, down in the meadow the other day,
    a gathering flowers both fine and gay,
A gathering flowers both red and blue,
    I little thought what love can do.

I leaned my back up against some oak
    thinking that he was a trusty tree;
But first he bended and then he broke;
    and so did my false love to me.
A ship there is and she sails the sea,
    she's loaded deep as deep can be,
But not so deep as the love I'm in:
    I know not if I sink or swim.

O, love is handsome and love is fine,
    and love's a jewel while it is new,
But when it is old, it groweth cold,
    and fades away like morning dew.

RENOUNCEMENT

Alice Meynell

I must not think of thee; and, tired yet strong,
    I shun the love that lurks in all delight -
    The thought of thee - and in the blue Heaven's height,
And in the dearest passage of a song.

Oh, just beyond the thoughts that throng fairest
    This breast, the thought of thee waits hidden, yet bright;
    But it must never, never come in sight;
I must stop short of thee the whole day long.

But when sleep comes to close each difficult day,
    When night gives pause to the long watch I keep,
        And all my bonds I needs must loose apart,
Must doff my will as raiment laid away, -
    With the first dream that comes with the first sleep
        I run, I run, I am gathered to thy heart.

THE ALMOND TREE

Jon Stallworthy

At seven-thirty
the visitors' bell
scissored the calm
of the corridors.
The doctor walked with me
to the slicing doors.

His hand upon my arm,
his voice – I have to tell
you – set another bell
beating in my head:
your son is a mongol
the doctor said.

You turn to the window for the first
    time.
I am called to the cot
to see your focus shift,
take tendril-hold on a shaft
of sun, explore its dusty surface, climb
to an eye you cannot

meet. You have a sickness they cannot
    heal,
the doctors say: locked in
your body you will remain.
Well, I have been locked in mine.
We will tunnel each other out. You seal
the covenant with a grin.

In the days we have known one another,
my little mongol love,
I have learnt more from your lips
than you will from mine perhaps:
I have learnt that to live is to suffer,
to suffer is to live.

DANTE CALLED YOU BEATRICE

Paul Potts

I have never had a sexual desire in my life in which all my other desires have not been wrapped up, and this is rare in a man. This is not quite factually true, but it contains the atmosphere of truth. It was true of Shelley; there is a Greek word for it, which I can never pronounce, let alone spell.

This attitude is quite usual in all women who are matured at all. There are very few men in the world to whom a relationship with a woman is the most important thing in their lives; I am one. To most women it is the mainspring of their whole existence. But to men, if they are artists their work comes first. If they are business men their careers. If they are Bohemians their leisure and their pleasure, which might be sex or it might even be a glass of beer. To me life is more important than fame, people than drink, friendship than success, happiness than pleasure, people than things. Living is talking, having is being with. Given a temperament like that, the main street of such a man's life is the knowing of the woman he loves. If that woman doesn't happen to love him, it quite simply means that he has failed to find a place in which to live ... Actually, in point of fact, to be practical, there is nothing to be done if you are in love with someone who does not love you. There is only one honest thing to do, that is to go away. Go to another country, to another town, to another world. Go, go anywhere, but in life's name, go. The only useful thing that a woman can do for a man who loves her this deeply is to love him equally in return. What else does he want?

MAN'S SEARCH FOR MEANING

Viktor E. Frankl

We stumbled on in the darkness, over big stones and through large puddles, along the one road leading from the camp. The accompanying guards kept shouting at us and driving us with the butts of their rifles. Anyone with very sore feet supported himself on his neighbour's arm. Hardly a word was spoken; the icy wind did not encourage talk. Hiding his mouth behind his upturned collar, the man marching next to me whispered suddenly: 'If our wives could see us now! I do hope they are better off in their camps and don't know what is happening to us.'

That brought thoughts of my own wife to mind. And as we stumbled on for miles, slipping on icy spots, supporting each other time and again, dragging one another up and onward, nothing was said, but we both knew: each of us was thinking of his wife. Occasionally I looked at the sky, where the stars were fading and the pink light of the morning was beginning to spread behind a dark bank of clouds. But my mind clung to my wife's image, imagining it with an uncanny acuteness. I heard her answering me, saw her smile, her frank and encouraging look. Real or not, her look was then more luminous than the sun which was beginning to rise.

A thought transfixed me: for the first time in my life I saw the truth as it is set into song by so many poets, proclaimed as the final wisdom by so many thinkers. The truth – that love is the ultimate and the highest goal to which man can aspire. Then I grasped the meaning of the greatest secret that human poetry and human thought and belief have to impart: *The salvation of man is through love and in love.* I understood how a man who has nothing left in this world still may know bliss, be it only for a brief moment, in the contemplation of his beloved. In a position of utter desolation, when man cannot express himself in positive action, when his only achievement may consist in enduring his sufferings in the right way – an honourable way – in such a position man can, through loving contemplation of the image he carries of his beloved, achieve fulfilment.

For the first time in my life I was able to understand the meaning of the words, 'The angels are lost in perpetual contemplation of an infinite glory.'

In front of me a man stumbled and those following him fell on top of him. The guard rushed over and used his whip on them all. Thus my thoughts were interrupted for a few minutes. But soon my soul found its way back from the prisoner's existence to another world, and I resumed talk with my loved one: I asked her questions, and she answered; she questioned me in return, and I answered.

'Stop!' We had arrived at our work site. Everybody rushed into the dark hut in the hope of getting a fairly decent tool. Each prisoner got a spade or a pickaxe.

'Can't you hurry up, you pigs?' Soon we had resumed the previous day's positions in the ditch. The frozen ground cracked under the point of the pickaxes, and sparks flew. The men were silent, their brains numb.

My mind still clung to the image of my wife. A thought crossed my mind: I didn't even know if she were still alive. I knew only one thing – which I have learned well by now: Love goes very far beyond the physical person of the beloved. It finds its deepest meaning in his spiritual being, his inner self. Whether or not he is actually present, whether or not he is still alive at all, ceases somehow to be of importance.

I did not know whether my wife was alive, and I had no means of finding out (during all my prison life there was no outgoing or incoming mail); but at that moment it ceased to matter. There was no need for me to know; nothing could touch the strength of my love, my thoughts, and the image of my beloved. Had I known then that my wife was dead, I think that I would still have given myself, undisturbed by that knowledge, to the contemplation of her image, and that my mental conversation with her would have been just as vivid and just as satisfying. 'Set me like a seal upon thy heart, love is as strong as death.'

MR AND MRS SCHARANSKY

Jeannette Kupfermann, Sunday Times, 1984

Mrs Avital Scharansky, wife of the imprisoned Soviet dissident Anatoly Scharansky, has managed to keep alive the spirit of her marriage for a decade, despite the fact she was only officially Anatoly's wife for one day. Their love affair had lasted three years – they met in Moscow while she was an art student, he a mathematician – but she was expelled from Russia the day after the wedding. Both had applied for exit visas together. Hers was granted and she assumed he would soon follow. But the authorities would not let Anatoly go, even though he was not even under arrest for the first couple of years . . . In 1975, he was sentenced to three years in a Soviet prison and ten years in a labour camp. In prison, systematic starvation resulted in severe weight loss, illness and near blindness.

'Last summer, when it looked like his release was imminent, I went and bought a flat in Jerusalem. I arranged things in it especially for his comfort – things I knew he would like and need . . .' But the summer passed, he was not released after all, and Avital went back to live with friends.

How does a beautiful young woman, in the prime of her life, cope without a man? Has she never been tempted to start life with someone else?

She looked shocked and slightly hurt: 'I never feel separated from him – somehow we're always together. I never feel alone' . . . Avital has received only two letters in seven years from Anatoly, and each time he has had to go on hunger strike to get them out.

'He pays for these letters with his body,' she told me, 'and the authorities know that our relationship gives him strength: they will do anything to undermine it. It's like Kafka – but it must be very hard for you to understand.'

The letters make poignant reading.

'You don't need to worry that I shall not recognize you,' he wrote to her in October 1978, 'Mama sent me your picture with friends in Jerusalem in the summer of 1978. I constantly compare that photo of you with the picture from Ista taken in the summer of 1974. You have lost a lot of weight. You are visibly tired. Naturally something has changed; but that something is that wisdom which was given to us by these bitter years of our life and which added to your youth and beauty, my beloved wife.'

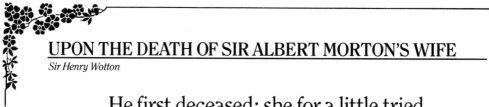

UPON THE DEATH OF SIR ALBERT MORTON'S WIFE

Sir Henry Wotton

He first deceased; she for a little tried
To live without him, liked it not, and died.

A SPACE IN THE AIR

Jon Silkin

The first day he had gone
I barely missed him. I was glad almost he
 had left
Without a bark or flick of his tail,
I was content he had slipped

Out into the world. I felt,
Without remarking, it was nearly a relief
From his dirty habits. Then, the second
Day I noticed the space

He left behind him. A hole
Cut out of the air. And I missed him
 suddenly,
Missed him almost without knowing
Why it was so. And I grew

Afraid he was dead, expecting death
As something I had grown used to. I was
 afraid
The clumsy children in the street
Had cut his tail off as

A souvenir of the living and
I did not know what to do. I was fearing
Somebody had hurt him. I called his
 name
But the hole in the air remained.

I have grown accustomed to death
Lately. But his absence made me sad,
I do not know how he should do it
But his absence frightened me.

It was not only his death I feared,
Not only his but as if all of those
I loved, as if all those near me
Should suddenly go

Into the hole in the light
And disappear. As if all of them should
 go
Without barking, without speaking,
Without noticing me there

But go; and going as if
The instrument of pain were a casual
 thing
To suffer, as if they should suffer so,
Casually and without greatness,

Without purpose even. But just go.
I should be afraid to lose all those
 friends like this.
I should fear to lose those loves. But
 mostly
I should fear to lose you.

If you should go
Without affliction, but even so, I should
 tear
The rent you would make in the air
And the bare howling

Streaming after your naked hair.
I should feel your going down more
 than my going down.
My own death I bear everyday
More or less

But your death would be something
 else,
Something else beyond me. It would not
 be
Your death or my death, love,
But our rose-linked dissolution.

So I feared his going,
His death, not our death, but a hint at
 our death. And I shall always fear
The death of those we love as
The hint of your death, love.

THE THREE WOMEN WHO WEPT

James Stephens

The first time they met he spoke to her. He plucked a handkerchief from somewhere and thrust it into her hand, saying –

'You have dropped this, I think' – and she had been too alarmed to disown it.

It was a mighty handkerchief. It was so big that it would scarcely fit into her muff.

'It is a table-cloth,' said she, as she solemnly stuffed away its lengthy flaps. 'It is own,' she thought a moment later, and she would have laughed like a mad woman, only that she had no time, for he was pacing delicately by her side, and talking in a low voice that was partly a whisper and partly a whistle, and was entirely and disturbingly delicious.

The next time they met very suddenly. Scarcely a dozen paces separated them. She could see him advancing towards her, and knew by his knitted brows that he was searching anxiously for something to say. When they drew together he lifted his hat and murmured –

'How is your handkerchief to-day?'

The query so astonished her that (the verb is her own) she simply bawled with laughter. From that moment he treated her with freedom, for if once you laugh with a person you admit him to equality, you have ranked him definitely as a vertebrate, your hand is his by right of species, scarcely can you withhold even your lips from his advances.

Another, a strange, a fascinating thing, was that he was afraid of her. It was inconceivable, it was mad, but it was true. He looked at her with disguised terror. His bravado was the slenderest mask. Every word he said was uttered tentatively, it was subject to her approval, and if she opposed a statement he dropped it instantly and adopted her alternative as one adopts a gift. This astonished her who had been prepared to be terrified. He kept a little distance between them as he walked, and when she looked at him he looked away. She had a vision of herself as an ogre – whiskers sprouted all over her face, her ears bulged and swaggled, her voice became a cavernous rumble, her conversation sounded like fee-faw-fum – and yet, her brothers were not afraid of her in the least; they pinched her and kicked her hat.

He spoke (but always without prejudice) of the loveliest things imaginable – matters about which brothers had no conception, and for which they would not have any reverence. He said one day that the sky was blue, and, on looking, she found that it was so. The sky was amazingly blue. It had never struck her before, but there was a colour in the firmament before which one might fall down and worship. Sunlight was not the hot glare which it had been: it was rich, generous, it was inexpressibly beautiful. The colour and scent of flowers became more varied. The world emerged as from shrouds and cerements. It was tender and radiant, comeliness lived everywhere, and goodwill. Laughter! the very ground bubbled with it: the grasses waved their hands, the trees danced and curtsied to one another with gentle dignity, and the wind lurched down the path with its hat on the side of its head and its hands in its pockets, whistling like her younger brother.

And then he went away. She did not see him any more. He was not by the waterfall on the Dodder, nor hanging over the bear-pit in the Zoo. He was not in the chapel, nor on the pavement when she came out of a shop. He was not anywhere. She searched, but he was not anywhere. And the sun became the hot pest it had always been: the heavens were stuffed with dirty clouds the way a secondhand shop is stuffed with dirty bundles: the trees were hulking corner-boys with muddy boots: the wind blew dust into her eye, and her brothers pulled her hair and kicked her hat; so that she went apart from all these. She sat before the mirror regarding herself with woeful amazement.

'He was afraid of me!' she said.

And she wept into his monstrous handkerchief.

WHAT I BELIEVE

Malcolm Muggeridge

I recognize, of course, that any statement of belief from me is partly governed by the fact that I am old, and in a decade or so will be dead. In earlier years I should doubtless have expressed things differently. Now the prospect of death overshadows all. I am like a man on a sea voyage nearing his destination. When I embarked I worried about having a cabin with a porthole, whether I should be asked to sit at the captain's table, who were the more attractive and important passengers. All such considerations become pointless now that I shall soon disembark.

Since I do not believe that earthly life can bring lasting satisfaction, the prospect of death holds no terrors. But the world that I shall leave seems more beautiful than ever, especially its remoter parts: grass and trees, little streams and sloping hills, where the image of eternity is more clearly stamped than among streets and houses. Those I love I can love even more, since I have nothing to ask of them but their love; the passion to accumulate possessions, or to be noticed and important, is now too evidently absurd to be entertained.

A sense of how extraordinarily happy I have been, and of enormous gratitude to my creator, overwhelms me. I believe with a passionate unshakeable conviction that life is a blessed gift; that the spirit which animates it is one of love not hate, of light not darkness.

Since I believe also that life is benevolently, not malevolently, conceived, then I know that when these eyes see no more and this mind thinks no more, and this hand now writing is inert, I shall find what lies beyond similarly benevolent. If that is nothing, then for nothingness I offer thanks; if it is another mode of existence, then for that likewise, I offer thanks.

AS I WALKED FORTH

Anon

As I walked forth one Summer's day
To view the meadows green and gay,
A pleasant bower I espied,
Standing fast by the river side;
And in't a maiden I heard cry:
Alas, alas, there's none ere lov'd as I.

Then round the meadow did she walk
Plucking each flower by the stalk,
Such flow'rs as in the meadow grew,
The dead man's thumb, an hearb all blew;
And as she pul'd them still cri'd she:
Alas, alas, there's none ere lov'd as I.

The flowers of the sweetest scent
She bound about with knotty bents,
And as she bound them up in bands,
She wept, she sigh'd and she wrong her hands:
Alas, alas, cri'd she,
Alas, alas, there's none ere lov'd as I.

When she had fil'd her apron full
Of such green things as she could cull;
The green things serv'd her for her bed,
The flowers were the pillows for her head;
Then down she lay'd her, Ne'er word more did speak,
Alas, alas, with love her heart did break.

THE LOVER BIDS
HIS HEART BE ABSENT

Gerald Bullett

Because I love her,
The sky is dark above her.
Because I find her fair,
There is menace in the very air.
A single leaf of the tree
Is not more frail than she,
Whose every breath
Draws her, because I love her,
nearer death.
So, heart, absent you from me now, that I,
Lest the beloved die,
May feign I do not love her.

THE ETERNAL YEAR

Karl Rahner

God's silence in this world is nothing but the earthly appearance of the eternal word of his love.

Our dead imitate this silence. Thus, through silence, they speak to us clearly. They are nearer to us than through all the audible words of love and closeness. Because they have entered into God's life, they remain hidden from us. Their words of love do not reach our ears because they have blended into one with the joyous word of his boundless love. They live with the boundlessness of God's life and with his love, and that is why their love and their life no longer enter the narrow room of our present life. We live a dying life. That is why we experience nothing of the eternal life of the holy dead, the life that knows no death. But just in this very way, they also live for us and with us. For their silence is their loudest cry because it is the echo of God's silence. It is in unison with God's word that it speaks to us . . . The dead are silent because they live, just as our noisy chatter is supposed to make us forget that we are dying. Their silence is the word of their love for us, the real message that they have for us. By this word they are really near to us, provided only that we listen to this soundless word and understand it, and not drown it out through the noise of our everyday life.

They are near us together with the silent God, the God of the silent dead, the living God of the living. He calls out to us through his silence, and they, by their silence, summon us into God's life.

Let us therefore be mindful of our dead, our living. Our love for them, our loyalty to them is the proof of our faith in him, the God of everlasting life. Let us not ignore the silence of the dead, the silence that is the most ardent word of their love. This, their most ardent word, accompanies us today and everyday, for they have gone away from us in order that their love, having gone into God, may be all the closer to us . . . Our living who are with the God of life cannot forget us dead. God has granted our living everything, for he has given them himself. But he goes further and also grants them this favour: that their silence will become the most eloquent word of their love for us, the word that will accompany our love home to them, into their life and their light. . . . all our memories and all our prayers are only the echo of the words of love that the holy living, in the silence of their eternity, softly and gently speak into our heart. Hidden in the peace of the eternal God, filled with his own bliss, redeemed for eternity, permeated with love for us that can never cease, they utter the prayer of their love for us: 'Lord, grant eternal rest (and life) to them whom we love – as never before – in your love. Grant it to them who still walk the hard road of pilgrimage, which is nonetheless the road that tends to us and to your eternal light. We, although silent, are now closer to them than ever before, closer than when we were sojourning and struggling along with them on earth. Grant to them, too, Lord, eternal rest, and may your perpetual light shine on them as on us. May it shine on them now as the light of faith, and then in eternity, as the light of blessed life.'

BEASTLY BEATITUDES OF BALTHAZAR B.

J. P. Donleavy

In the misty Belfast morning I took a taxi. Out through the smoky streets. The driver said he would ask his wife if he could drive me to Fermanagh. And he read a newspaper while drawn up by the side of the road. And I in this early afternoon went past the gate once held open on a broken hinge and now closed and padlocked. I stepped on stones and climbed over a broken part of the wall. And walked lost for a while. Brambles scratching through my trousers. To think I am here in trespass. Something I would never do. And look for where the land rises crowned by a wood. Cross this pasture. I know where I am. She lies just up there in the trees. Look down as I walk over her grass. And through the little irongate in the wall. I come here to say hello and not goodbye. A piece of granite stands tall and plain. Next to another half its size. Two words make your name. And underneath the years that lived your life. Primroses and violets grow here where you lie. You will never go away. See all of you through the tears that cover my eyes. Wind blows in the yew. Soft red berries dropped with a green shadowy seed. The musty smell of boxwood. When you looked at me and I looked back we each said all our words. It matters only what private things we know and have never spoken. Or will ever speak. Take up the years that come. To carry you with me wherever I go. Face any loneliness. Know I'm not alone. You the only one I ever told about my lost little boy who was my first son. Wish I could blow hoots from the hollow of my hand and make the owls answer back. Tonight I will be in Dublin. From the train through Dundalk. I'll walk across Trinity in the morning. Around its flat green velvet squares. See you again as you passed beneath my windows. I'll look from the roadway where your bedroom window was and at the house in which I first heard you speak to me. Never to know all those suffering creatures your hand and voice gave comfort in hospital. Putting bravery in old men in fear of death. And these tears that fall from me, they'll help your grass to grow. Goodbye Fitzdare. Goodbye.

   The day windy as I went out to Collinstown. And the plane rose in the sky over Dublin south towards London. I could see along the coast and count the towns, Dalkey, Bray and Greystones. And the train we took through tunnels and up on cliffs looking down on a wintry shore in summer. Leave Ireland now. With part of it mine. Where it has your grave.

THIS YEAR I SHALL LOVE THE RAIN

Mary Morison Webster

This year I shall love the rain,
And the dark leaves underfoot,
And the rose tree stripped to its root,
And the wind on my window pane.

Because love is gone at length,
I shall love the desolate winter,
The frost's unyielding splinter,
And the long night's terrible strength.

TIMELESS TALES OF GODS AND HEROES

Edith Hamilton

Where Orpheus first met and how he wooed the maiden he loved, Eurydice, we are not told, but it is clear that no maiden he wanted could have resisted the power of his song. They were married, but their joy was brief. Directly after the wedding as the bride walked in a meadow with her bridesmaids, a viper stung her and she died. Orpheus's grief was overwhelming. He could not endure it. He determined to go down to the world of death and try to bring Eurydice back.

He took the fearsome journey to the underworld. There he struck his lyre, and at the sound all that vast multitude were charmed to stillness. The ruler of Hades drew near to listen with his queen. No one under the spell of his voice could refuse him anything. He

> Drew iron tears down Pluto's cheek,
> And made Hell grant what Love did seek.

They summoned Eurydice and gave her to him, but upon one condition: that he would not look back at her as she followed him, until they had reached the upper world. So the two passed through the great doors of Hades to the path which would take them out of the darkness, climbing up and up. He knew that she must be just behind him, but he longed unutterably to give one glance to make sure. But now they were almost there, the blackness was turning grey; now he had stepped out joyfully into the daylight. Then he turned to her. It was too soon; she was still in the cavern. He saw her in the dim light, and he held out his arms to clasp her; but on the instant she was gone. She had slipped back into the darkness. All he heard was one faint word, 'Farewell.'

MESSAGES

Francis Thompson

What shall I your true-love tell,
   Earth-forsaking maid?
What shall I your true-love tell,
   When life's spectre's laid?

'Tell him that, our side the grave,
   Maid may not conceive
Life should be so sad to have,
   That's so sad to leave!'

What shall I your true-love tell,
   When I come to him?
What shall I your true-love tell –
   Eyes growing dim!

'Tell him this, when you shall part
   From a maiden pined;
That I see him with my heart,
   Now my eyes are blind.'

What shall I your true-love tell?
   Speaking-while is scant.
What shall I your true-love tell,
   Death's white postulant?

'Tell him – love, with speech at strife,
   For last utterance saith:
I, who loved with all my life,
   Love with all my death.'

ANNABEL LEE

Edgar Allan Poe

It was many and many a year ago
In a kingdom by the sea,
That a maiden there lived whom you
     may know
By the name of Annabel Lee,
And this maiden she lived with no other
     thought
Than to love and be loved by me.

For I was a child and she was a child,
In this kingdom by the sea:
But we loved with a love that was more
     than love -
I and my Annabel Lee:
With a love that the winged seraphs of
     heaven
Coveted her and me.

And this is the reason that, long ago,
(In this kingdom by the sea)
A wind blew out of a cloud,
Chilling my Annabel Lee:
So that her high-born kinsmen came
And bore her away from me,
To shut her up in a sepulcher
In this kingdom by the sea.

And the angels, not half so happy in
     heaven,
Went envying her and me -
Yes - that was the reason (as all men
     know,
In this kingdom by the sea)
That the wind came out of the cloud by
     night,

Chilling my Annabel Lee
That the wind came out of the cloud by
　　night,
Killing my Annabel Lee

But our love it was stronger by far than
　　the love
Of those who were older than we –
Of many far wiser than we –
Of many far wiser than we.
And neither the angels in heaven above,
Nor the demons down under the sea,
Can ever dissever my soul from the soul

Of the beautiful Annabel Lee

And the moon never beams, without
　　bringing me dreams
Of the beautiful Annabel Lee;
And the stars never rise, but I feel the
　　bright eyes
Of the beautiful Annabel Lee;
And all through the night, I lie down by
　　the side
Of my darling, my life and my bride,
In her sepulcher there by the sea,
In her tomb by the sounding sea.

RIDERS IN THE CHARIOT
Patrick White

Mrs Godbold walked by the greenish light of early darkness. A single tram spat violet sparks into the tunnel of brown flannel. Barely clinging to its curve, its metal screeched anachronism. But it was only as she waited at a crossing, watching the stream churn past, that dismay overtook Mrs Godbold, and she began to cry. It seemed as if the group of figures huddled on the bank was ignored not so much by the traffic as by the strong, undeviating flood of time. There they waited, the pale souls, dipping a toe timidly, again retreating, secretly relieved to find their fellows caught in a similar situation, or worse, for here was one who could not conceal her suffering.

The large woman was simply standing and crying, the tears running out at her eyes and down her pudding-coloured face. It was at first fascinating, but became disturbing to the other souls-in-waiting. They seldom enjoyed the luxury of watching the self-exposure of others. Yet, this was a crying in no way convulsed. Soft and steady, it streamed out of the holes of the anonymous woman's eyes. It was, it seemed, the pure abstraction of gentle grief.

The truth of the matter was: Mrs Godbold's self was by now dead, so she could not cry for the part of her which lay in the keeping of the husband she had just left.

She cried, rather, for the condition of men, for all those she had loved, burningly, or at a respectful distance, from her father, seated at his bench in his prison of flesh, and her own brood of puzzled little girls, for her former mistress, always clutching at the hem and finding it come away in her hand, for her fellow initiates, the mad woman and the Jew of Sarsaparilla, even for the blackfellow she had met at Mrs Khalil's, and then never again, unless by common agreement in her thoughts and dreams. She cried, finally, for the people beside her in the street, whose doubts she would never dissolve in words, but understood, perhaps, from those she had experienced.

THE MAKING OF A MIND

Pierre Teilhard de Chardin

Death surrenders us totally to God; it makes us enter into him; we must, in return, surrender ourselves to death with absolute love and self-abandonment – since, when death comes, all we can do is to surrender ourselves completely to the domination and guidance of God . . . I feel that there'd be something to say about the joy (the healthy joy) of death, about its harmony in life, about the intimate connexion (and at the same time the barrier) between the world of the dead and the world of the living, about the unity of both in one and the same cosmos. Death has been treated too much as a subject for melancholy reflexion, or as an occasion for self-discipline, or as a rather hazy theological entity . . . What we have to do is to see it in its time context, see it as an active reality, as one more phase, in a world and a 'becoming' that are those of our own experience.

MADAME BOVARY
Gustave Flaubert

Next day was a day of mourning to Emma. Everything seemed wrapped in a drifting, clinging darkness, and sorrow sank deep in her soul with a muffled wailing, like the winter wind in a derelict château. It was the spell cast by the departed, the lassitude that follows the event, the pain caused by any accustomed motion breaking off or prolonged vibration abruptly ceasing.

Sombrely melancholy, numbly despairing as when she had returned from La Vaubyessard with the dance-tunes whirling in her head, she now saw a taller, handsomer, a more delightful, and a vaguer Léon. He was far away, and yet he had not left her, he was here still, his shadow seemed to linger on the walls. She could not take her eyes from the carpet on which he had walked, the chairs in which he had sat. The river still flowed by, pushing its little waves along the slippery bank. Many a time they had strolled beside it, listening to that same murmuring of the water over the mossy pebbles. The fine sunny days they had had! The lovely afternoons, alone together in the shade at the bottom of the garden! He used to read aloud to her, perched on a footstool of dry sticks, bareheaded, while the cool breeze off the meadows fluttered the pages of his book and the nasturtiums round the arbour . . . He was gone – her only joy in life, her only hope of happiness! Why had she not seized that happiness when it offered? Why had she not held it, knelt to it, when it threatened to fly away? She cursed herself for not having given Léon her love. She thirsted for his lips. An impulse seized her to run after him, to throw herself into his arms and say 'It is I! I am yours!' But at once Emma felt dismayed at the difficulties of such an undertaking; and the vanity of the hope served but to intensify the desire.

From that moment her remembrance of Léon became the centre of her discontent; it crackled there more fiercely than a fire left burning in the snow by travellers in the Russian steppes. She ran to it, huddled herself against it, carefully stirred it when it flagged, and cast about for fresh fuel to revive it; and all that the distant past or the immediate present could offer, all she felt and all she fancied, her sensual longings that now melted into air, her plans for happiness that creaked like dead branches in the wind, her sterile virtue, her fallen hopes and her domestic martyrdom – anything and everything she gathered up and used to feed her grief.

IF I SHOULD GO BEFORE THE REST OF YOU
Joyce Grenfell

If I should go before the rest of you,
Break not a flower nor inscribe a stone.
Nor when I'm gone speak in a Sunday
    voice,
But be the usual selves that I have
    known.

Weep if you must,
Parting is hell,
But life goes on,
So sing as well.

ABSENCE

Elizabeth Jennings

I visited the place where we last met.
Nothing was changed, the gardens were
    well-tended,
The fountains sprayed their usual steady
    jet;
There was no sign that anything had
    ended
And nothing to instruct me to forget.

The thoughtless birds that shook out of
    the trees,
Singing an ecstasy I could not share,
Played cunning in my thoughts. Surely
    in these
Pleasures there could not be a pain to
    bear
Or any discord shake the level breeze.

It was because the place was just the
    same
That made your absence seem a savage
    force,
For under all the gentleness there came
An earthquake tremor: fountain, birds
    and grass
Were shaken by my thinking of your
    name.

A GRIEF OBSERVED

C. S. Lewis

There is, hidden or flaunted, a sword between the sexes till an entire marriage reconciles them. It is arrogance in us to call frankness, fairness, and chivalry 'masculine' when we see them in a woman; it is arrogance in them, to describe a man's sensitiveness or tact or tenderness as 'feminine'. But also what poor, warped fragments of humanity most mere men and mere women must be to make the implications of that arrogance plausible. Marriage heals this. Jointly the two become fully human. 'In the image of God created He *them.*' Thus, by a paradox, this carnival of sexuality leads us out beyond our sexes.

And then one or other dies. And we think of this as love cut short; like a dance stopped in mid career or a flower with its head unluckily snapped off – something truncated and, therefore, lacking its due shape. I wonder. If, as I can't help suspecting, the dead also feel the pains of separation (and this may be one of their purgatorial sufferings), then for both lovers, and for all pairs of lovers without exception, bereavement is a universal and integral part of our experience of love. It follows marriage as normally as marriage follows courtship or as autumn follows summer. It is not a truncation of the process but one of its phases; not the interruption of the dance, but the next figure. We are 'taken out of ourselves' by the loved one while she is here. Then comes the tragic figure of the dance in which we must learn to be still taken out of ourselves though the bodily presence is withdrawn, to love the very Her, and not fall back to loving our past, or our memory, or our sorrow, or our relief from sorrow, or our own love.

RIDERS TO THE SEA

John M. Synge

MAURYA: Bartley will be lost now, and let you call in Eamon and make me a good coffin out of the white boards, for I won't live after them. I've had a husband, and a husband's father, and six sons in this house – six fine men, though it was a hard birth I had with every one of them and they coming to the world – and some of them were found and some of them were not found, but they're gone now the lot of them . . . There were Stephen and Shawn were lost in the great wind, and found after in the Bay of Gregory of the Golden Mouth, and carried up the two of them on one plank, and in by that door.
[*She pauses for a moment, the girls start as if they heard something through the door that is half open behind them.*]
NORA [*in a whisper*]: Did you hear that, Cathleen? Did you hear a noise in the north-east?
CATHLEEN [*in a whisper*]: There's someone after crying out by the seashore.
MAURYA [*continues without hearing anything*]: There was Sheamus and his father, and his own father again, were lost in a dark night, and not a stick or sign was seen of them when the sun went up. There was Patch after was drowned out of a curagh that turned over. I was sitting here with Bartley, and he a baby lying on my two knees, and I seen two women, and three women, and four women coming in, and they crossing themselves and not saying a word. I looked out then, and there were men coming after them, and they holding a thing in the half of a red sail, and water dripping out of it – it was a dry day, Nora – and leaving a track to the door.
[*She pauses again with her hand stretched out towards the door. It opens softly and old women begin to come in, crossing themselves on the threshold, and kneeling down in front of the stage with red petticoats over their heads.*]
MAURYA [*half in a dream, to* CATHLEEN]: Is it Patch, or Michael, or what is it at all?
CATHLEEN: Michael is after being found in the far north, and when he is found there how could he be here in this place?
MAURYA: There does be a power of young men floating round in the sea, and what way would they know if it was Michael they had, or another man like him, for when a man is nine days in the sea, and the wind blowing, it's hard set his own mother would be to say what man was in it.
CATHLEEN: It's Michael, God spare him, for they're after sending us a bit of his clothes from the far north.
[*She reaches out and hands* MAURYA *the clothes that belonged to Michael.* MAURYA *stands up slowly, and takes them in her hands.* NORA *looks out.*]
NORA: They're carrying a thing among them, and there's water dripping out of it and leaving a track by the big stones.
CATHLEEN [*in a whisper to the women who have come in*]: Is it Bartley it is?
ONE OF THE WOMEN: It is, surely, God rest his soul.
[*Two younger women come in and pull out the table. Then men carry in the body of* BARTLEY, *laid on a plank, with a bit of a sail over it, and lay it on the table.*]
CATHLEEN [*to the women as they are doing so*]: What way was he drowned?
ONE OF THE WOMEN: The grey pony knocked him over into the sea, and he was washed out where there is a great surf on the white rocks.
[MAURYA *has gone over and knelt down at the head of the table. The women are*

keening softly and swaying themselves with a slow movement. CATHLEEN *and* NORA *kneel at the other end of the table. The men kneel near the door.]*

MAURYA [*raising her head and speaking as if she did not see the people around her*]: They're all gone now, and there isn't anything more the sea can do to me . . . I'll have no call now to be up crying and praying when the wind breaks from the south, and you can hear the surf is in the east, and the surf is in the west, making a great stir with the two noises, and they hitting one on the other. I'll have no call now to be going down and getting Holy Water in the dark nights after Samhain, and I won't care what way the sea is when the other women will be keening. [*To* NORA.] Give me the Holy Water, Nora; there's a small sup still on the dresser.

[NORA *gives it to her.*]

MAURYA [*drops Michael's clothes across* BARTLEY'*s feet, and sprinkles the Holy Water over him*]: It isn't that I haven't prayed for you, Bartley, to the Almighty God. It isn't that I haven't said prayers in the dark night till you wouldn't know what I'd be saying; but it's a great rest I'll have now, and it's time, surely. It's a great rest I'll have now, and great sleeping in the long nights after Samhain, if it's only a bit of wet flour we do have to eat, and maybe a fish that would be stinking . . . They're all together this time, and the end is come. May the Almighty God have mercy on Bartley's soul, and on Michael's soul, and on the souls of Sheamus and Patch, and Stephen and Shawn [*bending her head*]; and may He have mercy on my soul, Nora, and on the soul of every one is left living in the world.

AE FOND KISS

Robert Burns

Ae fond kiss, and then we sever!
Ae fareweel, and then for ever!
Deep in hert-wrung tears I'll pledge
    thee,
Waring sighs and groans I'll wage thee.

Had we never loved sae kindly,
Had we never loved sae blindly,
Never met – or never perted,
We had ne'er been broken-herted.

Fare thee weel, thou first and fairest!
Fare thee weel, thou best and dearest!
Thine be ilka joy and treasure,
Peace, Enjoyment, Love and Pleasure.

Ae fond kiss, and then we sever;
Ae fareweel, alas, for ever!
Deep in hert-wrung tears I'll pledge
    thee,
Waring sighs and groans I'll wage thee.

BENNY
Brigid Marlin

> Some are born to sweet delight;
> Some are born to endless night.
> *William Blake*

At puberty, Benny's illness became more acute, and he suffered a complete mental breakdown. Life became intolerable at home with him as he became more and more difficult. Because he was so big and strong my fear of mental illness was united with a very real physical fear. To my horror I found that I seemed to have come to the end of my feeling of love for my son. What kept me going was a sense of duty. At last he was taken into a mental home, and I went to visit him regularly; always with a feeling of dread. This unhappiness threatened to engulf me until I made a bargain with myself. I would do all that needed to be done for my boy, and do it to the best of my ability. Then in between times I would try to put him out of my mind and live as joyfully as I could for the other children and myself. After all, Benny would derive no profit from my misery. As time went by I found that I had stumbled on a source of great help for myself. These moments of joy in everyday life gave me the strength I needed to cope with the bad times.

One day I got a telephone call from the hospital. Benny had taken a massive overdose. I got there as quickly as possible. In the intensive care unit, he looked so beautiful. All the anger and depression had left his face. On the tenth day he moved his hand, and they knew that he would come round. The next day he looked at me and smiled. All my love for him, so long buried, came flooding back. As I came in the next morning he opened his arms in a hug. He was my loving little child again, as he had been as a toddler. On the following day he could speak and he croaked in a whisper, 'You know the books of C. S. Lewis? I've been there. I've been on a planet like Narnia.' He had wanted to stay but he had to go back to earth. He said, 'If I get better I want to help people. Sick people like me.' As he regained his strength, the horror came. Like a rat reboarding a salvaged ship, his illness returned. One morning he threatened me with a knife. After we had been so loving together, the shock was so great that I had not the power to bear it. I began to sob and could not stop. Benny apologised and began to weep too; but he could not help the changes in his personality. He was back to being depressed and hostile. We went back and forth to the doctor; he was given different drugs; we were back in the old situation.

When the unbearable happens, and still has to be borne, one comes to the end of one's resources. I went to a priest friend for help. He said, 'God did not promise that we would not suffer but He did promise that we would not be alone. He is always with you if you turn to Him.'

From that moment when things got bad I would withdraw whenever I could for a moment and say to God, 'I can't bear this; please bear it for me.' Always I got enough support to carry on. Sometimes only enough for one more step; and sometimes so much inner peace and help that I could say with St Augustine, 'Not I that live; but Thou that livest in me.' God could go on loving Benny through me, when I seemed to have reached the end of my natural love.

Benny finally died. That he should have lived only to suffer is still a question for me. But somewhere once I heard it expressed that man on earth represents Christ, and suffering man represents Christ's suffering. And so it could be that these sick and despised ones represent Christ standing before Pilate, mocked, scourged and mute. Silent before Pilate's question: 'What is Truth?'

WILL YOU REMEMBER . . .?

John Gawsworth

When I have turned to death's more chill
    embrace,
Braving the coldest kisses of decay,
Will you remember how you held my
    face
Breathing love-life into poor mortal
    clay?

Will you remember how I loved you
    then? -
Earth being hallowed wheresoe'er you
    trod,
Life being that eternal moment when
We kist for all time, finding Love as
    God . . .

Yes, I believe, unclouded in your mind
The memory of our past love will
    remain:
Whilst I, poor dreamer, never shall I find
Such lips as yours again.

THE SPECIAL YEARS

Val Doonican

The very next day, he appeared to have improved and talked to me in a perfectly normal and sane manner. When the time was up and I made signs of leaving, he took my hand and said, 'Now listen, boy.'

I slowly sank back on to the side of the bed and looked at him. By this time, by the way, the illness had distorted his face and mouth to such an extent that the hospital staff had bandaged his entire face and head, except for his eyes and nose which were still visible.

He continued, 'You know that I'm going to die, don't you?'

I nodded, 'Yes, mammy told me your sickness was serious.'

'Well,' he said, 'I think I will be going pretty soon, so I wanted to say something to you.' He paused and then went on, 'Now, you think I'm a great fella, don't you?'

'Yes, I do!' I answered without a second's hesitation.

'Before I go,' he went on, 'I think it's only fair that I should tell you that I'm not! You see, when I'm gone I know that in time people will say to you that your father was no good. Well, nothing would please me more than for you to say, "Yes, I know that, he told me himself".'

That is still the most wonderful thing I've ever known anybody do in my life: he made sure that the deep love I had for him could never be damaged.

THE BRIDGE OF SAN LUIS REY

Thornton Wilder

But Doña Clara stood in the door as the Abbess talked to them, the lamp placed on the floor beside her. Madre María stood with her back against a post; the sick lay in rows gazing at the ceiling and trying to hold their breaths. She talked that night of all those out in the dark (she was thinking of Esteban alone, she was thinking of Pepita alone) who had no one to turn to, for whom the world perhaps was more than difficult, without meaning. And those who lay in their beds there felt that they were within a wall that the Abbess had built for them; within all was light and warmth, and without was the darkness they would not exchange even for a relief from pain and from dying. But even while she was talking, other thoughts were passing in the back of her mind. 'Even now,' she thought, 'almost no one remembers Esteban and Pepita but myself. Camila alone remembers her Uncle Pio and her son; this woman, her mother. But soon we shall die and all memory of those five will have left the earth, and we ourselves shall be loved for a while and forgotten. But the love will have been enough; all those impulses of love return to the love that made them. Even memory is not necessary for love. There is a land of the living and a land of the dead, and the bridge is love, the only survival, the only meaning.'

BLESSINGS

Mary Craig

Our friends were so sure that Paul's death was an unqualified blessing that I felt guilty about the grief I felt for him. I knew that what hurt most in the general rejoicing was the assumption that Paul's life had been a useless irrelevance, a disaster best forgotten.

To me it did not seem like that. Yes, I was glad he was dead. But at the same time, I owed him an incalculable debt. If our value as human beings lies in what we do for each other, Paul had done a very great deal: he had, at the very last, opened the eyes of his mother to the suffering that was in the world, and had brought her to understand something of the redemptive force it was capable of generating. I had been broken, but I had been put together again, and I had met many who bore far more inspiring witness than I to the strength inherent in the mending process. What Paul had done for me was to challenge me to face up to the reality of my own situation; and he had handed me a key to unlock reserves buried so deep I hadn't suspected their existence.

Self-knowledge comes to us only in the dark times, when we are stripped of illusion and naked to truth. If Paul had helped me towards even a little understanding, how could I agree that he had lived to no purpose? He had taught me a lesson, quite unwittingly, and now that he was no longer there, I owed it to him not to forget.

POSTSCRIPT FOR GWEN

Alun Lewis

If I should go away,
Beloved, do not say
'He has forgotten me'.
For you abide,
A singing rib within my dreaming side;
You always stay.
And in the mad tormented valley
Where blood and hunger rally
And death the wild beast is uncaught,
   untamed,
Our soul withstands the terror
And has its quiet honour
Among the glittering stars your voices
   named.

LUCY

William Wordsworth

She dwelt among the untrodden ways
   Beside the springs of Dove,
A Maid whom there were none to praise
   And very few to love:

A violet by a mossy stone
   Half hidden from the eye!
- Fair as a star, when only one
   Is shining in the sky.

She lived unknown, and few could know
   When Lucy ceased to be;
But she is in her grave, and, oh,
   The difference to me!

THE PROPHET

Kahlil Gibran

And when Almustafa entered into the city all the people came to meet him, and they
   were crying out to him as with one voice.
And the elders of the city stood forth and said:
Go not yet away from us.
A noontide have you been in our twilight, and your youth has given us dreams to
   dream.
No stranger are you among us, nor a guest, but our son and our dearly beloved.
Suffer not yet our eyes to hunger for your face.

And the priests and the priestesses said unto him:
Let not the waves of the sea separate us now, and the years you have spent in our
   midst become a memory.
You have walked among us a spirit, and your shadow has been a light upon our faces.
Much have we loved you. But speechless was our love, and with veils has it been
   veiled.
Yet now it cries aloud unto you, and would stand revealed before you.
And ever has it been that love knows not its own depth until the hour of separation.

Love
and
God

Love and God

The worship of God is not a rule of safety – it is an adventure of the spirit, a flight after the unattainable.

So wrote A. N. Whitehead in *Science and the Modern World*. To be sure, God is not attainable in the sense that in this life man cannot see God and live. But despite the hazards and the knowledge that it is a terrible thing to fall into the hands of the living God, man ploughs on in a kind of blind searching, and there is a reassuring sense in which we can't get away from the Absolute, the personal loving energy at the heart of all creation. For 'in Him we live, move and have our being'.

One of the signs of loving is the wanting to be known. The doctrine of the Trinity is about God's innermost life. He revealed that mystery to us because He loves us and wants to be known by us. Usually it takes more than a dry text-book knowledge of Him, veiled in dogmatic formulae to stir our love. The ways in which we first become aware of this passionately loving God, ways through which He becomes alive and immediate for us, are many and varied. A moment comes when He is no longer 'out there' but 'the greatest of present facts'. Sometimes, as in my own case at the age of twenty, it is the awakening of a deep human love that unexpectedly brings about the beginning of this particular spiritual consciousness. And if we guard and nourish this new-found awareness in faith we are on a voyage of discovery.

Some years ago during a patch of depression, the sort where you feel 'wedged' and can't foresee ever being able to free yourself, a verse from Scripture came to my rescue: 'Let me be glad and rejoice in your love.' I came to see that it also had a deeper meaning than merely: 'Let me rejoice in the fact that you, God, love me.' It dawned on me that it means: 'Let me rejoice in the love you have for yourself – that intense love between the Father and the Son which is inherent in the Blessed Trinity.' Nothing can assail the perfection of this total bliss, and that was and still is a liberating realisation. Being glad and rejoicing in God's own love in Himself, one's miseries dissipate like vapour.

This is not to say that God is not also focused on us, His creatures. Loving us in no way lessens the triune love.

> Elijah went into the cave and spent the night in it. Then he was told, 'Go and stand on the mountain before the Lord.' Then the Lord himself went by. There came a mighty wind, so strong it tore the mountains and shattered the rocks before the Lord. But the Lord was not in the wind. After the wind came an earthquake. But the Lord was not in the earthquake. After the earthquake came a fire. But the Lord was not in the fire. And after the fire there came the whisper of a gentle breeze. And when Elijah heard this, he covered his face with his cloak and went out and stood at the entrance of the cave (1 Kings 19: 9, 11-13, *Jerusalem*).

The key to the understanding I have of this passage lies in verse 21 of Psalm 108 which says: 'Yahweh, no love so tender as Yours.' I like to think that 'the whisper of a gentle breeze' spoke to the prophet Elijah, as it does to me, of the penetrating tenderness of God's love.

Age to age you're still the same,
By the power of the name,
El-Shaddai, El-Shaddai,
Erkamkana Adonai,
I will praise you till I die,
El-Shaddai, El-Shaddai,
El-Shaddai.

PRAYER
Swami Abhishiktananda

Prayer is the smile, the look of the eyes which conveys to any other man the greetings of a heart, which tells him, unknown as he may be and met by chance in a public place or vehicle, that he is not really a stranger, but is recognized and loved as a brother ... It is an act of prayer and contemplation to look at the sun, at the stars, at the sky, when faith reveals in them the presence and love of the creator, since through them he prepared the earth to be the cradle of mankind and the place of the Incarnation. Is it not through the sun particularly, through its light and heat, that life was made possible here below for the children of the father, and especially for his first born, the Lord Jesus, who blessed the sun for ever with his divine glance?

IN TIME OF TEMPTATION
Ladislaus Boros

God created the world out of pure love, since he can do nothing other than love ... God can't force us to meet him in love. He stands there defenceless, full of goodness and understanding.

LOVE
C. S. Lewis

It is probably impossible to love any human being 'too much'. We may love him too much in proportion to our love of God but it is the smallness of our love for God, not the greatness of our love for the man, that constitutes the inordinacy.

REVELATIONS OF DIVINE LOVE
Julian of Norwich

He showed me a little thing, the size of a hazelnut in the palm of my hand, and it was as round as a ball. I looked at it with my mind's eye and I thought, 'What can this be?' And answer came, 'It's all that is made.' I marvelled that it could last, for I thought it might have crumbled to nothing, it was so small. And the answer came into my mind, 'It lasts and ever shall because God loves it.' And all things have being through the love of God.

Peace and love are always alive in us, but we are not always alive to peace and love.

And so I saw full surely that before ever God made us he loved us. And this love has never faded nor ever shall. And in this love he has done all his works, and in this love he has made all things profitable to us, and in this love our life is everlasting. In our making we had beginning, but the love in which he made us was in him from without beginning, in which love we have our beginning.

LADY WHOSE GRAVE I OWN

(for Simone Weil, died 1943) Leslie Paul

Ah Simone, was it love of God that struck you down,
Or the more compelling love of men?
There is an affliction of the body too,
    which trembles in the eyes,
In the palm's sweat, the straight but straying hair,
Unguarded tongue and makes unlovely
That which loves with such a fever
The body's broken by a rigor.
If you had loved less, cared less!
Caring and loving all
Made certain that slow fall.

It is the mark of the afflicted that
Their own sin's endurable
But they carry into heartbreak
The burden of another's pain,
And more, they are all gravity,
So stricken
Beyond all earthly hope is their despair.

The complacency of the unafflicted
Is more than they can stomach
The adolescent sniggers, the casual lovers
In shadowed arcades, the faceless men in faultless suits
In the Kremlins of power.

And so, Simone, lady whose grave I own,
The migraine, the nausea without cessation,
The Solesmes masses beating on the brain,
The iron will to shrug off so much suffering –
This we know.

But tell us godly Simone
Of the waiting till the Saviour came again.

Was this the real affliction,
The cross you had to bear,
That you were simply what you were?

THE GREEN STICK

Malcolm Muggeridge

Surveying the abysmal chasm between my certainty that everything human beings tried to achieve was inadequate to the point of being farcical, that mortality itself was a kind of gargoyle joke, and my equal certainty that every moment of every day was full of enchantment and infinitely precious; that human love was the image vouchsafed us of God's love irradiating the whole universe; that, indeed, embedded in each grain of sand was eternity, to be found and explored, as geologists explored the antiquity of fossils through their markings – surveying this chasm, yawning in its vastness to the point of inducing total insanity, tearing us into schizophrenic pieces, I grasped that over it lay, as it were, a cable-bridge, frail, swaying, but passable. And this bridge, this reconciliation between the black despair of lying bound and gagged in the tiny dungeon of the ego, and soaring upwards into the white radiance of God's universal love – this bridge was the Incarnation, whose truth expresses that of the desperate need it meets. Because of our physical hunger we know there is bread; because of our spiritual hunger we know there is Christ.

SILENT MUSIC

William Johnston

Christian contemplation is the answer to a call and the response to a vision. One cannot embark on the journey until one has heard the voice or glimpsed the footprints of the ox. In other words there is an initial awakening. One stops in one's tracks, amazed by the realization that one is loved. Christian contemplation begins with the belief, the conviction, the experience of God's love for me. It never starts with vigorous efforts on my part; it does not manifest itself through active energy; it does not begin with my violently drumming up some powerful love for God and man. This is stated explicitly by John: 'In this is love, not that we loved God but that he loved us' (1 John 4:10). This love powerfully experienced has been compared to the call of the good shepherd inviting us to enter the sheepfold.

Now this call is creative. It creates a response, an interior movement, a motion of love that necessarily expresses itself in an altered state of consciousness. So deep is the call and so interior is my response that a new level of awareness is opened up and I enter into a changed environment. Christian contemplation is the experience of being loved and of loving at the most profound level of psychic life and of spirit.

This love is not directed to some imaginary world of escape beyond the senses. Rather does it go out to the great reality of the cosmic, risen Christ who loves me and whom I love. This is the Christ who is before our very eyes and ears and hearts and whose glory is all around us because he is 'the mountains, the solitary wooded valleys, strange islands . . . silent music', and the people I meet every day.

SOME REFLECTIONS ON THE LOVE OF GOD

Simone Weil

Religion teaches that God created finite beings of different degrees of mediocrity. We human beings are aware that we are at the extreme limit, the limit beyond which it is no longer possible to conceive or to love God. Below us there are only the animals. We are as mediocre and as far from God as it is possible for creatures endowed with reason to be. This is a great privilege. It is for us, if he wants to come to us, that God has to make the longest journey. When he has possessed and won and transformed our hearts it is we in our turn who have to make the longest journey in order to go to him. The love is in proportion to the distance.

It was by an inconceivable love that God created beings so distant from himself. It is by an inconceivable love that he comes down so far as to reach them. It is by an inconceivable love that they then ascend so far as to reach him. It is the same love. They can only ascend by the same love which God bestowed on them when he came down to seek them. And this is the same love by which he created them at such a great distance from him. The Passion is not separable from the Creation. The Creation itself is a kind of passion. My very existence is like a laceration of God, a laceration which is love. The more mediocre I am, the more obvious is the immensity of the love which maintains me in existence.

The evil which we see everywhere in the world in the form of affliction and crime is a sign of the distance between us and God. But this distance is love and therefore it should be loved. This does not mean loving evil, but loving God through the evil. When a child in his play breaks something valuable, his mother does not love the breakage. But if later on her son goes far away or dies she thinks of the incident with infinite tenderness because she now sees it only as one of the signs of her child's existence. It is in this way that we ought to love God through everything good and everything evil, without distinction. If we love only through what is good, then it is not God we are loving but something earthly to which we give that name. We must not try to reduce evil to good by seeking compensations or justifications for evil. We must love God through the evil that occurs, solely because everything that actually occurs is real and behind all reality stands God. Some realities are more or less transparent; others are completely opaque; but God is behind all of them, without distinction. It is for us simply to keep our eyes turned towards the point where he is, whether we can see him or not. If there were no transparent realities we should have no idea of God. But if all realities were transparent it would not be God but simply the sensation of light that we would be loving. It is when we do not see God, it is when his reality is not sensibly perceptible to any part of our soul, that we have to become really detached from the self in order to love him. That is what it is to love God.

MISTER GOD, THIS IS ANNA
Fynn

'Fynn, Mister God doesn't love us.' She hesitated. 'He doesn't really, you know, only people can love. I love Bossy, but Bossy don't love me. I love the pollywogs, but they don't love me. I love you, Fynn, and you love me, don't you?'

I tightened my arm about her.

'You love me because you are people. I love Mister God truly, but he don't love me.'

It sounded to me like a death knell. 'Damn and blast', I thought. 'Why does this have to happen to people? Now she's lost everything.' But I was wrong. She had got both feet planted firmly on the next stepping-stone.

'No,' she went on, 'no, he don't love me, not like you do, it's different, it's millions of times bigger.'

I must have made some movement or noise for she levered herself upright and sat on her haunches and giggled. Then she launched herself at me and undid my little pang of hurt, cut out the useless spark of jealousy with the delicate sureness of a surgeon.

'Fynn, you can love better than any people that ever was, and so can I, can't I? But Mister God is different. You see, Fynn, people can only love outside and can only kiss outside, but Mister God can love you right inside, and Mister God can kiss you right inside, so it's different. Mister God ain't like us; we are a little bit like Mister God, but not much yet.'

It seemed to me to reduce itself to the fact that we were like God because of some similarities but God was not like us because of our difference. Her inner fires had refined her ideas, and like some alchemist she had turned lead into gold. Gone were all the human definitions of God, like Goodness, Mercy, Love and Justice, for these were merely props to describe the indescribable.

'You see, Fynn, Mister God is different from us because he can finish things and we can't. I can't finish loving you because I shall be dead millions of years before I can finish, but Mister God can finish loving you, and so it's not the same kind of love, is it?'

BROTHERLY LOVE
Louis Evely

It is by brotherly love that the Son's return is made ready.

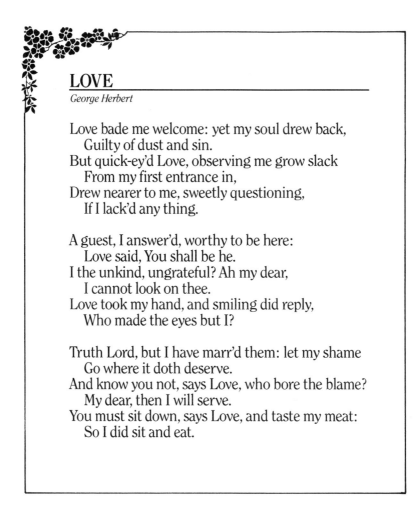

LOVE
George Herbert

Love bade me welcome: yet my soul drew back,
    Guilty of dust and sin.
But quick-ey'd Love, observing me grow slack
    From my first entrance in,
Drew nearer to me, sweetly questioning,
    If I lack'd any thing.

A guest, I answer'd, worthy to be here:
    Love said, You shall be he.
I the unkind, ungrateful? Ah my dear,
    I cannot look on thee.
Love took my hand, and smiling did reply,
    Who made the eyes but I?

Truth Lord, but I have marr'd them: let my shame
    Go where it doth deserve.
And know you not, says Love, who bore the blame?
    My dear, then I will serve.
You must sit down, says Love, and taste my meat:
    So I did sit and eat.

PRAYER
Attributed to Bede Jarrett

We seem to give them back to you, O God, who gave them to us. For as you did not lose them in giving, so do we not lose them by their return. Not as the world gives do you give, O lover of men. For what you give you take not away. And what is yours is ours also if we are yours. For love is immortal and life is eternal and death is only an horizon, and an horizon is nothing save the limit of our sight.

Lift us up, strong Son of God, that we may see further. Cleanse our eyes that we may see more clearly. Draw us closer to you that we may know ourselves to be closer to those we love. And while you prepare a home for us, prepare us also for that happy place that with you (and with them) we may live and reign for ever and ever.

Amen.

THE SIGN OF JONAS

Thomas Merton

God never does things by halves. He does not sanctify us patch upon patch. He takes our whole life and our whole being and elevates it to a supernatural level, transforms it completely from within, and leaves it exteriorly what it is: ordinary.

To love God is everything. And Love is enough. Nothing else is of any value except insofar as it is transformed and elevated by the charity of Christ. But the smallest thing, touched by charity, is immediately transfigured and becomes sublime.

SELF-ABANDONMENT TO DIVINE PROVIDENCE

Jean-Pierre de Caussade

If we are able to envisage each moment as the manifestation of the Will of God, we shall find in it all that our heart can desire. For what can there be more reasonable, more perfect, more divine than the Will of God? Can its infinite value increase through differences of time, place and circumstance? If you are given the secret of finding it at every moment in every event, you possess all that is most precious and worthy in your desires. What do you desire, holy souls? Let yourselves go, carry your longings beyond all measures and limits, dilate your hearts to an infinite extent, I have enough to fill them: there is no moment at which I cannot make you find all that you can desire.

The present moment is always full of infinite treasures, it contains far more than you have the capacity to hold. Faith is the measure, you will find in the present moment according as you believe. Love also is the measure: the more your heart loves, the more it desires, and the more it desires the more it finds. The Will of God presents itself at each instant like an immense ocean which the desire of your heart cannot empty, although it will receive of that ocean the measure to which it can extend itself by faith, confidence and love. The whole of the created universe cannot fill your heart which has a greater capacity than everything else that is not God. The mountains which alarm your eyes, are but atoms to the heart. The Divine Will is an abyss the opening of which is the present moment. Plunge into this abyss and you will find it even deeper than your desires.

HYMN OF LOVE

1 Corinthians 13

If I speak with the eloquence of men and of angels, but have no love, I become no more than blaring brass or crashing cymbal. If I have the gift of foretelling the future and hold in my mind not only all human knowledge but the very secrets of God, and if I also have that absolute faith which can move mountains, but have no love, I amount to nothing at all. If I dispose of all that I possess, yes, even if I give my own body to be burned, but have no love, I achieve precisely nothing.

This love of which I speak is slow to lose patience – it looks for a way of being constructive. It is not possessive: it is neither anxious to impress nor does it cherish inflated ideas of its own importance.

Love has good manners and does not pursue selfish advantage. It is not touchy. It does not keep account of evil or gloat over the wickedness of other people. On the contrary, it is glad with all good men when Truth prevails.

Love knows no limit to its endurance, no end to its trust, no fading of its hope; it can outlast anything. It is, in fact, the one thing that still stands when all else has fallen.

GITANJALI

Rabindranath Tagore

Have you not heard his silent steps? He comes, comes, ever comes.

Every moment and every age, every day and every night he comes, comes, ever comes.

Many a song have I sung in many a mood of mind, but all their notes have always proclaimed, 'He comes, comes, ever comes.'

In the fragrant days of sunny April through the forest path he comes, comes, ever comes.

In the rainy gloom of July nights on the thundering chariot of clouds he comes, comes, ever comes.

In sorrow after sorrow it is his steps that press upon my heart, and it is the golden touch of his feet that makes my joy to shine.

IN LOVING THEE
A. Samaan-Hanna

In loving Thee,
I have loved suns that rise
And the surprise
That only stars and wings can bring
To eyes
never inured
To the lure of Thy wonders.

THIRSTING FOR GOD
Psalm 42

My soul is thirsting for God,
The God of my life;
When can I enter and see
The face of God?

VOYAGE TO VENUS
C. S. Lewis

In the plan of the Great Dance plans without number interlock, and each movement becomes in its season the breaking into flower of the whole design to which all else had been directed. Thus each is equally at the centre and none are there by being equals, but some by giving place and some by receiving it, the small things by their smallness and the great by their greatness, and all the patterns linked and looped together by the unions of a kneeling with a sceptred love. Blessed be He!

He has immeasurable use for each thing that is made, that His love and splendour may flow forth like a strong river which has need of a great water-course and fills alike the deep pools and the little crannies, that are filled equally and remain unequal; and when it has filled them brim full it flows over and makes new channels. We also have need beyond measure of all that He has made. Love me, my brothers, for I am infinitely necessary to you and for your delight I was made. Blessed be He!

He has no need at all of anything that is made. An eldil is not more needful to Him than a grain of the Dust: a peopled world no more needful than a world that is empty: but all needless alike, and what all add to Him is nothing. We also have no need of anything that is made. Love me, my brothers, for I am infinitely super-fluous, and your love shall be like His, born neither of your need nor of my deserving, but a plain bounty. Blessed be He!

A NEW SONG
St Augustine of Hippo

We are told to sing to the Lord a new song.
A new man knows a new song.
A song is a thing of joy and,
If we think about it, a thing to love.
So the man who has learned to love a new life
Has learned to sing a new song.
For a new man, a new song and the
New Testament all belong to the same kingdom.

THE WAY OF A PILGRIM

Translated from Russian by R. M. French

I felt as it were hungry for prayer, an urgent need to pour out my soul in prayer, and I had not been in quiet nor alone for forty-eight hours. I felt as though there were in my heart a sort of flood struggling to burst out and flow through all my limbs. To hold it back caused me severe, even if comforting, pain in the heart, a pain which needed to be calmed and satisfied in the silence of prayer. And now I saw why those who really practise interior self-acting prayer have fled from the company of men and hidden themselves in unknown places. I saw further why the venerable Isikhi called even the most spiritual and helpful talk mere idle chatter if there were too much of it, just as Ephrem the Syrian says, 'Good speech is silver, but silence is pure gold.'

I went along without hurrying for about a month with a deep sense of the way in which good lives teach us and spur us on to copy them. I read *The Philokalia* a great deal, and there made sure of everything I had told the blind man of prayer. His example kindled in me

zeal and thankfulness and love for God. The Prayer of my heart gave me such consolation that I felt there was no happier person on earth than I, and I doubted if there could be greater and fuller happiness in the kingdom of Heaven. Not only did I feel this in my own soul, but the whole outside world also seemed to me full of charm and delight. Everything drew me to love and thank God; people, trees, plants, animals. I saw them all as my kinsfolk, I found on all of them the magic of the Name of Jesus. Sometimes I felt as light as though I had no body and was floating happily through the air instead of walking. Sometimes when I withdrew into myself I saw clearly all my internal organs, and was filled with wonder at the wisdom with which the human body is made. Sometimes I felt as joyful as if I had been made Tsar. And at all such times of happiness, I wished that God would let death come to me quickly, and let me pour out my heart in thankfulness at His feet in the world of spirits.

THE CLOUD OF UNKNOWING

Anon

Lift up your heart to God with humble love: and mean God himself, and not what you get out of him. Indeed, hate to think of anything but God himself, so that nothing occupies your mind or will but only God. Try to forget all created things that he ever made, and the purpose behind them, so that your thought and longing do not turn or reach out to them either in general or in particular. Let them go, and pay no attention to them. It is the work of the soul that pleases God most. All saints and angels rejoice over it, and hasten to help it on with all their might. All the fiends, however, are furious at what you are doing, and try to defeat it in every conceivable way. Moreover, the whole of mankind is wonderfully helped by what you are doing, in ways you do not understand ... But now you will ask me, 'How am I to think of God himself, and what is he?' and I cannot answer you except to say 'I do not know!' For with this question you have brought me into the same darkness, the same cloud of unknowing where I want you to be! For though we through the grace of God can know fully about all other matters, and think about them – yes, even the very works of God himself – yet of God himself can no man think. Therefore I will leave on one side everything I can think, and choose for my love that thing which I cannot think! Why? Because he may well be loved, but not thought. By love he can be caught and held, but by thinking never ... Should any thought arise and obtrude itself between you and the darkness, asking what you are seeking, and what you are wanting, answer that it is God you want: 'Him I covet, him I seek, and nothing but him.'

Should he (the thought) ask, 'What is this God?' answer that it is the God who made you and redeemed you, and who has, through his grace, called you to his love. 'And', tell him, 'you do not even know the first thing about him.'

A TOUCH OF GOD

Maria Boulding

When I was a child my father's hands meant a great deal to me. They were the most beautiful hands I have ever seen: large, beautifully shaped, strong, very sensitive and kind. I have many memories of clinging to them, but one recurrent joy stands out, that of being bathed by him as a small child. He used to run plenty of water into the bath, and make it very soapy and then put his child in. He scorned flannels, sponges and other impediments and did the whole job with his hands, caressing the child all over. At the time I simply enjoyed it with a mixture of sensuous delight and love; since then the memory of it has become for me a kind of sacrament of resting in the loving, cleansing, healing, creative hands of God.

LEAD KINDLY LIGHT

John Henry Newman

Lead, Kindly Light, amid the encircling
    gloom,
        Lead Thou me on!
The night is dark, and I am far from
    home -
        Lead Thou me on!
Keep Thou my feet; I do not ask to see
The distant scene, - one step enough for
    me.

So long Thy power hath blest me, sure it
    still
        Will lead me on,
O'er moor and fen, o'er crag and torrent,
    till
        The night is gone;
And with the morn those angel faces
    smile
Which I have loved long since, and lost
    awhile.

FEAR NOT

Isaiah 43

Fear not for I have redeemed you. I have called you by your name. You are mine.
When you pass through the waters, I will be with you, and through the rivers, they
shall not overwhelm you, because you are precious in my eyes and I love you . . . I
have graven you on my hands . . . It is the Lord who speaks . . .

IN A COUNTRY CHURCH

R. S. Thomas

To one kneeling down no word came,
Only the wind's song, saddening the lips
Of the grave saints, rigid in glass;
Or the dry whisper of unseen wings,
Bats not angels, in the high roof.

Was he balked by silence? He kneeled
   long,
And saw love in a dark crown
Of thorns blazing, a winter tree
Golden with fruit of a man's body.

LA JOIE DE CONNAÎTRE

Pierre Termier

I believe that there have always been worshippers, suppliants and lovers ... That has been enough for God. As the earth turns round the sun times without number, many crimes are committed on its surface, many bestial cries, shouts of grief and despair, even blasphemies rise from this strangely fated planet to the horror-stricken skies: but the holy murmur from retreats where simple good men are praying, easily drown the shouting and the blasphemy; and the smoke of sacrifice, a thin blue column rising into the calm air of dawn and dusk, bears a perfume so keen that it destroys the stench of crimes.

Love
and
Friendship

Love and Friendship

Oh, the comfort, the inexpressible comfort
of feeling safe with a person;
having neither to weigh thoughts nor
measure words,
but pour them all out, just as they are,
chaff and grain together,
Knowing that a faithful hand will take and
sift them,
keep what is worth keeping,
And then with the breath of kindness, blow
the rest away.

How beautifully this quote from George Eliot encapsulates the breadth and wonder of friendship! Sir Laurens van der Post in a TV interview published in *The Listener* stated that 'there is no love so good and so powerful as the one you find expressed in friendship'.

When I was first sent away to boarding-school I soon became aware, perhaps due to some measure of loneliness, of the enviable pairs of 'best friends' in my class. Deciding to do something about this lack in my own life at the time I settled on a particular girl whom I liked and, dispensing with any preamble, asked: 'Will you be my friend?' She looked at me, possibly not relishing the prospect, but successfully concealing the fact, and after a moment's silence replied: 'But sure, I'm Lita's friend.' End of exchange. It was clearly the wrong way of going about acquiring a friend. True friendship, while being selective, creeps up on us and cannot be established by edict. In passages I quote later on, John Dalrymple and Martin Buber each warn us against over-analysing or over-rationalising love and therefore friendships. Such matters are best left at the level of instinct, for when one becomes introspective about love, it can lose its freshness and become self-indulgent.

Our use of the word friend, as of the word love, is sometimes imprecise, often meaning merely an acquaintance or colleague. But a friend is more than just this. There are various levels of friendship and though one can have many friends only a few can be close. This is partly because friendships take up so much of our time and energy. When it comes to friendships we can so easily spread ourselves too thin. An intimate friendship implies a sharing, not only of interests but of values and the baring of one's inner self, which is always a risk. There are some people who are incapable of this and this must be why they never have close friends. Friendship or the capacity for it is a gift. I often think that relationships break up, not for lack of love, but for lack of friendship. In a society that is obsessed with the *instant,* from instant coffee to instant communication with TV-dinners thrown in, friendships and personal loyalties which need time to mature (and often grow at the cost of some pain) quickly become casualties. In earlier times perhaps the role of personal friendship was less vital than it is today when so many, especially young people, appear to suffer from the disorientating effect of modern fragmented society. In an earlier, more stable society the traditional support of a local, tightly knit and long-established community and the over-arching canopy of symbols supplied by a common faith, prevented widespread alienation and the sense of homelessness one finds in the uprooted and fast-changing society of today. Personal friendships counter this.

THE ANTHEAP

Doris Lessing

A child may say of a companion one day that he hates so and so, and the next: He is my friend. That is how a relationship is, shifting and changing, and children are kept safe in their hates and loves by the fabric of social life their parents make over their heads. And middle-aged people say: This is my friend, this is my enemy, including all the shifts and changes of feeling in one word, for the sake of an easy mind. In between these ages, at about twenty perhaps, there is a time when the young people test everything, and accept many hard and cruel truths about living, and that is because they do not know how hard it is to accept them finally, and for the rest of their lives. It is easy to be truthful at twenty.

But it is not easy at ten, a little boy entirely alone, looking at words like friendship. What, then, was friendship? Dirk was his friend, that he knew, but did he like Dirk? Did he love him? Sometimes not at all. He remembered how Dirk had said: 'I'll get you another baby buck. I'll kill its mother with a stone.' He remembered his feeling of revulsion at the cruelty. Dirk was cruel. But – and here Tommy unexpectedly laughed, and for the first time he understood Dirk's way of laughing. It was really funny to say that Dirk was cruel, when his very existence was a cruelty. Yet Mr Macintosh laughed in exactly the same way, and his skin was white, or rather, white browned over by the sun. Why was Mr Macintosh also entitled to laugh, with that same abrupt ugliness? Perhaps somewhere in the beginnings of the rich Mr Macintosh there had been the same cruelty, and that had worked its way through the life of Mr Macintosh until it turned into the cruelty of Dirk, the coloured boy, the half-caste? If so, it was all much deeper than differently coloured skins, and much harder to understand.

And then Tommy thought how Dirk seemed to wait always, as if he, Tommy, were bound to stand by him, as if this were a justice that was perfectly clear to Dirk; and he, Tommy, did in fact fight with Mr Macintosh for Dirk, and he could behave in no other way. Why? Because Dirk was his friend? Yet there were times when he hated Dirk, and certainly Dirk hated him, and when they fought they could have killed each other easily, and with joy.

Well, then? Well, then? What was friendship, and why were they bound so closely, and by what? Slowly the little boy, sitting alone on his antheap, came to an understanding which is proper to middle-aged people, that resignation in knowledge which is called irony. Such a person may know, for instance, that he is bound most deeply to another person, although he does not like that person, in the way the word is ordinarily used, or like the way he talks, or his politics, or anything else. And yet they are friends and will always be friends, and what happens to this bound couple affects each most deeply, even though they may be in different continents, or may never see each other again. Or after twenty years they may meet, and there is no need to say a word, everything is understood. This is one of the ways of friendship, and just as real as amiability or being alike.

Well, then? For it is a hard and difficult knowledge for any little boy to accept. But he accepted it, and knew that he and Dirk were closer than brothers and always would be so. He grew many years older in that day of painful struggle, while he listened to the mine-stamps saying gold, gold, and to the ants working away with their jaws to destroy the bench he sat on, to make food for themselves.

Next morning Dirk came to the shed, and Tommy, looking at him, knew that he, too, had grown years older in the months of working in the great pit. Ten years old – but he had been working with men and he was not a child.

THE LITTLE PRINCE

Antoine de Saint-Exupery

It was then that the fox appeared.

'Good morning,' said the fox.

'Good morning,' the little prince responded politely, although when he turned around he saw nothing.

'I am right here,' the voice said, 'under the apple tree.'

'Who are you?' asked the little prince, and added, 'You are very pretty to look at.'

'I am a fox,' the fox said.

'Come and play with me,' proposed the little prince. 'I am so unhappy.'

'I cannot play with you,' the fox said. 'I am not tamed.'

'Ah! Please excuse me,' said the little prince.

But, after some thought, he added:

'What does that mean – "tame"?'

'You do not live here,' said the fox. 'What is it that you are looking for?'

'I am looking for men,' said the little prince. 'What does that mean – "tame"?'

'Men,' said the fox. 'They have guns, and they hunt. It is very disturbing. They also raise chickens. These are their only interests. Are you looking for chickens?'

'No,' said the little prince. 'I am looking for friends. What does that mean – "tame"?'

'It is an act too often neglected,' said the fox. 'It means to establish ties.'

' "To establish ties?" '

'Just that,' said the fox. 'To me, you are still nothing more than a little boy who is just like a hundred thousand other little boys. And I have no need of you. And you, on your part, have no need of me. To you, I am nothing more than a fox like a hundred thousand other foxes. But if you tame me, then we shall need each other. To me, you will be unique in all the world. To you, I shall be unique in all the world . . . My life is very monotonous,' he said. 'I hunt chickens; men hunt me. All the chickens are just alike, and all men are just alike. And, in consequence, I am a little bored. But if you tame me, it will be as if the sun came to shine on my life. I shall know the sound of a step that will be different from all the others. Other steps send me hurrying back underneath the ground. Yours will call me, like music, out of my burrow. And then look: you see the grain-fields down yonder? I do not eat bread. Wheat is of no use to me. The wheat fields have nothing to say to me. And that is sad. But you have hair that is the colour of gold. Think how wonderful that will be when you have tamed me! The grain, which is also golden, will bring me back the thought of you. And I shall love to listen to the wind in the wheat . . .'

The fox gazed at the little prince, for a long time.

'Please – tame me!' he said.

MOTHER AND SON

Liam O'Flaherty

The mother sat on the doorstep, knitting in silence and watching him lovingly from under her long black eyelashes.

All her anger had vanished by now and she felt glad that she had thrust all the responsibility for punishment on to her long husband. Still, she wanted to be severe, and although she wanted to ask Stephen what he had been doing, she tried to hold her tongue. At last, however, she had to talk.

'What kept you, Stephen?' she said softly.

Stephen swallowed the last mouthful and turned around with his mug in his hand.

'We were only playing ball,' he said excitingly, 'and then Red Michael ran after us and chased us out of his field where we were playing. And we had to run an awful way; oh, a long, long way we had to run, over crags where I never was before.'

'But didn't I often tell you not to go into people's fields to play ball?'

'Oh, Mother, sure it wasn't me but the other boys that wanted to go, and if I didn't go with them they'd say I was afraid, and Father says I mustn't be afraid.'

'Yes, you pay heed to your father but you pay heed to your mother that has all the trouble with you. Now and what would I do if you fell running over the crags and sprained your ankle?'

And she put her apron to her eyes to wipe away a tear.

Stephen left his chair, came over to her and put his arms around her neck.

'Mother,' he said, 'I'll tell you what I saw on the crags if you promise not to tell Father about me being late and playing ball in Red Michael's field.'

'I'll do no such thing,' she said.

'Oh, do, Mother,' he said, 'and I'll never be late again, never, never, never.'

'All right, Stephen; what did you see, my little treasure?'

He sat down beside her on the threshold and, looking wistfully out into the sky, his eyes became big and dreamy and his face assumed an expression of mystery and wonder.

'I saw a great big black horse,' he said, 'running in the sky over our heads, but none of the other boys saw it but me, and I didn't tell them about it. The horse had seven tails and three heads and its belly was so big that you could put our house into it. I saw it with my two eyes. I did, Mother. And then it soared and galloped away, away ever so far. Isn't that a great thing I saw, Mother?'

'It is, darling,' she said dreamily, looking out into the sky, thinking of something with soft eyes. There was silence. Then Stephen spoke again without looking at her.

'Sure you won't tell on me, Mother?'

'No, treasure, I won't.'

'On your soul you won't?'

'Hush, little one. Listen to the birds. They are beginning to sing. I won't tell at all. Listen to the beautiful ones.'

They both sat in silence, listening and dreaming, both of them.

THE TOY HORSE
Valentine Iremonger

Somebody, when I was young, stole my toy horse,
The charm of my morning romps, my man's delight.
For two days I grieved, holding my sorrow like flowers
Between the bars of my sullen angry mind.

Next day I went out with evil in my heart,
Evil between my eyes and at the tips of my hands,
Looking for my enemy at the armed stations,
Until I found him, playing in his garden

With my toy horse, urgent in the battle
Against the enemies of his Unreason's land:
He was so happy, I gave him also
My vivid coloured crayons and my big glass marble.

THE VELVETEEN RABBIT

Margery Williams

'What is REAL?' asked the Rabbit one day, when they were lying side by side ... 'Does it mean having things that buzz inside you and a stick-out handle?'

'Real isn't how you are made,' said the Skin Horse. 'It's a thing that happens to you. When a child loves you for a long, long time, not just to play with, but REALLY loves you, then you become Real.'

'Does it hurt?' asked the Rabbit.

'Sometimes,' said the Skin Horse, for he was always truthful. 'When you are Real you don't mind being hurt.'

'Does it happen all at once, like being wound up,' he asked, 'or bit by bit?'

'It doesn't happen all at once,' said the Skin Horse. 'You become. It takes a long time. That's why it doesn't often happen to people who break easily, or have sharp edges, or who have to be carefully kept. Generally, by the time you are Real, most of your hair has been loved off, and your eyes drop out and you get loose in the joints and very shabby. But these things don't matter at all, because once you are Real you can't be ugly, except to people who don't understand.'

'I suppose you are Real?' said the Rabbit. And then he wished he had not said it, for he thought the Skin Horse might be sensitive. But the Skin Horse only smiled.

'The Boy's Uncle made me Real,' he said. 'That was a great many years ago; but once you are Real you can't become unreal again. It lasts for always.'

TWILIGHT

John Masefield

Twilight it is, and the far woods are dim,
    and the rooks cry and call.
Down in the valley the lamps, and the
    mist, and a star over all,
There by the rick, where they thresh, is
    the drone at an end,
Twilight it is, and I travel the road with
    my friend.

I think of the friends who are dead, who
    were dear long ago in the past,
Beautiful friends who are dead, though I
    know that death cannot last;
Friends with the beautiful eyes that the
    dust has defiled,
Beautiful souls who were gentle when I
    was a child.

AT FIRST SIGHT

Robert Graves

'Love at first sight,' some say, misnaming
Discovery of twinned helplessness
Against the huge tug of procreation.

But friendship at first sight? This also
Catches fiercely at the surprised heart
So that the cheek blanches and then
    blushes.

BETWEEN MAN AND MAN

Martin Buber

When I was eleven years of age, spending the summer on my grandparents' estate, I used, as often as I could do it unobserved, to steal into the stable and gently stroke the neck of my darling, a broad dapply-grey horse. It was not a casual delight but a great, certainly friendly, but also deeply stirring happening. If I am to explain it now, beginning from the still very fresh memory of my hand, I must say that what I experienced in touch with the animal was the Other, the immense otherness of the Other, which, however, did not remain strange iike the otherness of the ox and the ram, but rather let me draw near and touch it. When I stroked the mighty mane, sometimes marvellously smooth-combed, at other times just as astonishingly wild, and felt the life beneath my hand, it was as though the element of vitality itself bordered on my skin, something that was not I, was certainly not akin to me, palpably the other, not just another, really the Other itself; and yet it let me approach, confided itself to me, placed itself elementally in the relation of Thou and Thou with me. The horse, even when I had not begun by pouring oats for him into the manger, very gently raised his massive head, ears flicking, then snorted – quietly as a conspirator gives a signal meant to be recognisable only by his fellow-conspirator; and I was approved. But once – I do not know what came over the child, at any rate it was childlike enough – it struck me about the stroking, what fun it gave me, and suddenly I became conscious of my hand. The game went on as before, but something had changed, it was no longer the same thing. And the next day, after giving him a rich feed, when I stroked my friend's head he did not raise his head.

TORTILLA FLAT
John Steinbeck

Danny saw them coming, and he stood up and tried to remember the things he had to say. They lined up in front of him and hung their heads.

'Dog of dogs', Danny called them, and 'thieves of decent folks' other house,' and 'spawn of cuttlefish'. He named their mothers cows and their fathers ancient sheep.

Pilon opened the bag he held and exposed the ham sandwiches. And Danny said he had no more trust in friends, that his faith had been frostbitten and his friendship trampled upon. And then he began to have a little trouble remembering, for Pablo had taken two devilled eggs out of his bosom . . .

When the evening came, and it was dark, they went into the house and built a fire of cones in the airtight stove. Danny, in proof of his forgiveness, brought out a quart of grappa and shared its fire with his friends.

They settled easily into the new life. 'It is too bad Mrs Morales' chickens are all dead,' Pilon observed.

But even here was no bar to happiness. 'She is going to buy two dozen new ones on Monday,' said Danny.

Pilon smiled contentedly. 'Those hens of Mrs Soto's were no good,' he said. 'I told Mrs Soto they needed oyster shells, but she paid no attention to me.'

They drank the quart of grappa, and there was just enough to promote the sweetness of comradeship.

'It is good to have friends,' said Danny. 'How lonely it is in the world if there are no friends to sit with one and to share one's grappa.'

'Or one's sandwiches,' Pilon added quickly.

Pablo was not quite over his remorse, for he suspected the true state of celestial politics which had caused the burning of the house. 'In all the world there are few friends like thee, Danny. It is not given to many to have such solace.'

Before Danny sank completely under the waves of his friends, he sounded one warning. 'I want all of you to keep out of my bed,' he ordered. 'That is one thing I must have to myself.'

Although no one had mentioned it, each of the four knew they were all going to live in Danny's house.

Pilon sighed with pleasure. Gone was the worry of the rent; gone the responsibility of owing money. No longer was he a tenant, but a guest. In his mind he gave thanks for the burning of the other house.

'We will all be happy here, Danny,' he said. 'In the evenings we will sit by the fire and our friends will come in to visit. And sometimes maybe we will have a glass of wine to drink for friendship's sake.'

Then Jesus Maria, in a frenzy of gratefulness, made a rash promise. It was the grappa that did it, and the night of the fire, and all the devilled eggs. He felt that he had received great gifts, and he wanted to distribute a gift. 'It shall be our burden and our duty to see that there is always food in the house for Danny,' he declaimed. 'Never shall our friend go hungry.'

Pilon and Pablo looked up in alarm, but the thing was said; a beautiful and generous thing. No man could with impunity destroy it. Even Jesus Maria understood, after it was said, the magnitude of his statement. They could only hope that Danny would forget it.

'For,' Pilon mused to himself, 'if this promise were enforced, it would be worse than rent. It would be slavery.'

'We swear it, Danny!' he said.

They sat about the stove with tears in their eyes, and their love for one another was almost unbearable.

Pablo wiped his wet eyes with the back of his hand, and he echoed Pilon's remark. 'We shall be very happy living here,' he said.

THE SCENT OF THE ROSES

Thomas Moore

Farewell! but whenever you welcome the hour
That awakens the night-song of mirth in your bower,
Then think of the friend who once welcom'd it too,
And forgot his own grief to be happy with you.
His griefs may return, not a hope may remain
Of the few that have brighten'd his pathway of pain,
But he ne'er will forget the short vision that threw
Its enchantment around him, while ling'ring with you.

And still on that evening when pleasure fills up
To the highest top-sparkle each heart and each cup,
Where'er my path lies, be it gloomy or bright,
My soul, happy friends, will be with you that night;
Shall join in your revels, your sports, and your wiles,
And return to me, beaming all o'er with your smiles -
Too blest, if it tells me that, 'mid the gay cheer
Some kind voice had murmur'd, 'I wish he were here!'

Let Fate do her worst, there are relics of joy,
Bright dreams of the past, which she cannot destroy;
Which come in the night-time of sorrow and care,
And bring back the features that joy used to wear.
Long, long be my heart with such memories fill'd!
As the vase, in which roses have once been distill'd -
You may break, you may shatter the vase, if you will,
But the scent of the roses will hang round it still.

YOU NEEDED ME

Randy Goodrum

I cried a tear, you wiped it dry,
I was confused, you cleared my mind,
I sold my soul, you bought it back for
    me,
You held me up and gave me dignity,
Somehow you needed me.

You gave me strength to stand alone
    again
To face the world out on my own
    again ...

You held my hand when it was cold,
When I was lost you took me home,
You gave me hope when I was at the end
And turned my lies back into truth
    again,
You even called me 'Friend'.

DON'T WALK BEFORE ME

Albert Camus

Don't walk before me, I may not follow,
Don't walk behind me, I may not lead,
Just walk beside me, and be my friend.

FROM QUIET HOMES

Hilaire Belloc

From quiet homes and first beginning,
    Out to the undiscovered ends,
There's nothing worth the wear of winning,
    But laughter and the love of friends.

THE BLIND IN SOCIETY

Jacques Lusseyran

This is my story. I saw, saw with my eyes, until I was eight years old. For more than thirty-five years now I have been blind, completely blind. I know that this story, this experience, is my greatest happiness.

What thirty-seven years of blindness have taught me – I must admit – is to make great efforts. But they are much more than efforts; they are also discoveries.

Barely ten days after the accident that blinded me, I made the basic discovery. I am still entranced by it. The only way I can describe that experience is in clear and direct words. I had completely lost the sight of my eyes: I could not see the light of the world anymore. Yet the light was still there.

It was there. Try to imagine what surprise that must have been for a boy not yet eight years old. True, I could not see the light outside myself anymore, the light that illuminates objects, is associated with them, and plays on them. All the world around me was convinced that I had lost it for ever. But I found it again in another place. I found it in myself and what a miracle! – it was intact.

The second great discovery came almost immediately afterwards. There was only one way to see the inner light, and that was to love.

When I was overcome with sorrow, when I let anger take hold of me, when I envied those who saw, the light immediately decreased. Sometimes it even went out completely. Then I became blind. But this blindness was a state of not loving anymore, of sadness; it was not the loss of one's eyes.

I spoke to you of discoveries. This was one of them, and it was so great that a whole lifetime full of religion and morality is often not enough to enable others to make it . . . Blindness is my greatest happiness! It gives us a great opportunity, both through its disorder and through the order it creates.

The disorder is the prank it plays on us, the slight shift it causes. It forces us to see the world from another standpoint. This is a necessary disorder, because the principal reason for our unhappiness and our errors is that our standpoints are fixed.

As for the order blindness creates, it is the discovery of the constantly present creation. We constantly accuse the conditions of our lives. We call them incidents, accidents, illnesses, duties, infirmities. We wish to force our own conditions on life; this is our real weakness. We forget that God never creates new conditions for us without giving us the strength to meet them. I am grateful that blindness has not allowed me to forget this.

MR GILFIL'S LOVE-STORY

George Eliot

Animals are such agreeable friends – they ask no questions, they pass no criticisms.

THE ROCK OF DOUBT

Sydney Carter

So, we need our friends. One friend is enough to start with. By my neighbour or my wife, by my cat or toad or dog, even, I unlock what I carry in myself. Books, songs, pictures, trees are friends; I must choose them carefully, or I may unlock what is better left locked up. I carry for them, they carry for me, the keys of heaven and of hell . . . Love your neighbour as yourself: for yourself is in your neighbour. You can only find it through your neighbour. Do not think about God, for the moment: think about your deepest self, the self that you can only find by being with somebody else. That body does not have to be a human body: it may be the body of an animal, a piece of sculpture, or a star ten million miles away. It need not be tangible: it may take the form of a body made by sound, as in music, or a structure made of words. It may even seem to take the form of your own body, as in running, jumping, dancing, riding on a surf board or a horse. There is a kind of otherness in your own body; what comes from deep inside you might as well be coming from outside you. From deep inside you or from deep outside you, you come into contact with an otherness which is, yet is not, yourself.

   Words collapse in face of this experience: all they can do is to point towards it. Self and not-self intermingle all the time. You are your own neighbour, and your neighbour you. Love is where you feel, most sharply, the absurdity, the falsity of your position as a separated being. Yet, by this very separation, this absurdity, you are able to express what you could not express in any other way. By your very otherness, you are able to celebrate identity.

THE TASK

William Cowper

I would not enter on my list of friends,
(Though grac'd with polish'd manners and fine sense
Yet wanting sensibility) the man
Who needlessly sets foot upon a worm.

POEMS

Emily Dickinson

Elysium is as far as to
The very nearest room,
If in that room a friend await
Felicity or doom.

A SERMON IN RHYME

Daniel W. Hoyt

If you have a friend worth loving
Love him. Yes, and let him know
That you love him, ere life's evening
Tinge his brow with sunset glow.
Why should good words ne'er be said
Of a friend till he is dead?

A POISON TREE

William Blake

I was angry with my friend;
I told my wrath, my wrath did end.
I was angry with my foe;
I told it not, my wrath did grow.

COSTING NOT LESS THAN EVERYTHING

John Dalrymple

Love is immediate. It ends at people, not purely subjective intermediaries. Today it is fatally easy to become involved in subjective intermediaries instead of becoming involved in people. (We can spend our time analysing relationships and evaluating results instead of relating.) ... Knowing and loving people is like riding a bicycle. Too much looking down to see how one is doing and whether the machinery is working properly means that one will lose balance and fall off. The thing to do is to look where one wants to go and then go! It is better to go hard on a faulty bike than to sit looking at oneself on a perfect one ... Two knowledgeable Narcissi living in separate boxes and killing with science each approach from the other. They are off balance because they look at the bicycle so much that they forget to ride ... Exposure to others turns us away from analysis which tends to be narrowing, towards involvement in real people which is expanding. Those who give themselves over to this Spirit of love find themselves increasingly given over to other people in all their concreteness. In this way they find themselves turned outward from themselves and, having done so, find fulfilment. The fulfilment which Christ brought us was not, therefore, so much one which replenishes our minds with knowledge as one which replenishes our hearts with love.

THE FOUR LOVES

C. S. Lewis

Something which is going on at this moment in dozens of ward-rooms, bar-rooms, common-rooms, messes and golf-clubs – I prefer to call it companionship, or clubbableness . . . This companionship is, however, only the matrix of friendship. It is often called friendship, and many people when they speak of their 'friends' mean only their companions. But it is not Friendship in the sense I give to the word. By saying this I do not at all intend to disparage the merely clubbable relation. We do not disparage silver by distinguishing it from gold . . . Very few modern people think Friendship even a love at all . . . To the Ancients, Friendship seemed the happiest and most fully human of all loves; the crown of life and the school of virtue. The modern world, in comparison, ignores it . . . Friendship is in a sense not at all derogatory to it, the least natural of loves; the least instinctive, organic, biological, gregarious and necessary. It has least commerce with the nerves; there is nothing throaty about it; nothing that quickens the pulse or turns you red and pale. It is essentially between individuals; the moment two people are friends they have in some degree drawn apart together from the herd.

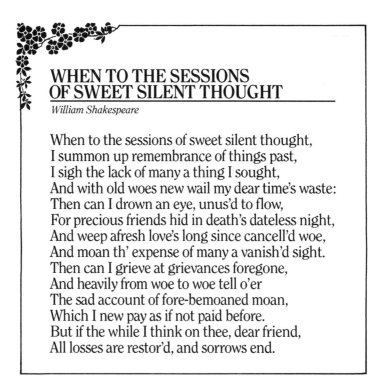

WHEN TO THE SESSIONS OF SWEET SILENT THOUGHT

William Shakespeare

When to the sessions of sweet silent thought,
I summon up remembrance of things past,
I sigh the lack of many a thing I sought,
And with old woes new wail my dear time's waste:
Then can I drown an eye, unus'd to flow,
For precious friends hid in death's dateless night,
And weep afresh love's long since cancell'd woe,
And moan th' expense of many a vanish'd sight.
Then can I grieve at grievances foregone,
And heavily from woe to woe tell o'er
The sad account of fore-bemoaned moan,
Which I new pay as if not paid before.
But if the while I think on thee, dear friend,
All losses are restor'd, and sorrows end.

SILENT MUSIC

William Johnston

At our present stage of evolution the men and women who go beyond the erotic and emotional to reach the spiritual core of another are probably few in number. And perhaps only the mystics (or those who aspire to mysticism) are capable of doing so. Yet the possibility is there. And the mystics are the greatest friends. If they are a married couple, they may express their love through sexual intercourse; if they are celibate, they practise restraint and renunciation. But in either case their love can be warm and growing and creative.

In this whole area, some of the richest and most challenging ideas flow from the pen of Teilhard de Chardin. Radically dedicated to celibacy, he yet had the most intimate spiritual relationships with both men and women friends; and he experienced in the depth of his being the creativity that is unleashed by such encounters. As always, he sees friendship and spiritual love in their cosmic setting. Woman leads man out of his cramping isolation, pointing the way to a universal love that encompasses mankind and the whole universe, leading on to God. Moreover, man-woman love is the force that builds the cosmos and stimulates the thrust of life towards ever more fullness of being. Teilhard willingly admits that his most cherished ideas came to birth under feminine influence with its tender inspiration . . . Woman leads man out of his isolation. This she does by teaching him how to love. Through her he learns what it means to be loved and to love; and such an experience is ultimately 'ecstatic'. It carries him beyond the barriers of self into a wider world where he meets his truest love, who is 'the mountains, the solitary wooded valleys, strange islands . . . silent music'.

In true friendship, then, we find a movement away from absorption towards universality, away from self-centredness towards cosmification. Here is a strange combination of affection and detachment, of sincere personal love for another and limitless personal love for the universe, of deep emotional attachment without self-centred clinging. And just as in the ascent of Mount Carmel one sometimes gets ecstatic glimpses of the summit, so, in the journey into the dark being of another, one may get fleeting glimpses of that other's personal core.

FRIENDSHIP

Ralph Waldo Emerson

The only way to have a friend is to be one.

DO YOU LISTEN – FOR LOVE?

Marjorie Shearer

The following dialogue occurs in the play, *The Curious Savage,* by John Patrick:

MRS SAVAGE: What's the matter, Fairy May?

FAIRY: Nothing. It's just that no one has said they loved me this livelong day.

MRS SAVAGE: I heard Florence say it at the dinner table.

FAIRY: Did she?

MRS SAVAGE: She said, 'Don't eat too fast.'

Sometimes we are timid about expressing the love we feel. For fear of embarrassing the other person – or ourselves – we hesitate to say the actual words, 'I love you.' So we try to communicate the idea in other ways: 'Take care' or 'Don't drive too fast.' As the perceptive Mrs Savage points out, such remarks carry the message of love: 'You are important to me. I care what happens to you. I don't want you to get hurt.'

But one has to *listen* for love. When a father tells his son to drive carefully, the son may think his dad implies that he hasn't sense enough to drive carefully. Instead of love, resentment flares, and both are bruised in the exchange.

Sometimes the explicit words are necessary, but the *manner* of saying things is even more important. A joyous insult carries more affection and warmth than sentiments expressed insincerely. A friendly grin and a hand extended are sacramental in nature: outward and visible signs of inward, spiritual grace. An impulsive hug says, 'I love you,' even though the words may come out, 'You old billygoat.'

Any expression of a person's concern for another says, 'I love you.' Sometimes the expression is clumsy. Sometimes we must look and listen very hard for the love it contains. At such times, when we listen intently, we are unconsciously expressing our own love, our concern for the other person. 'The first duty of love is to listen,' says theologian Paul Tillich.

We say, 'I love you,' in many ways: with valentines and birthday presents, with smiles and tears, with poems and cups of tea; sometimes by keeping our mouths shut, other times by speaking out, even brusquely; sometimes by gentleness, by listening, by thoughtfulness, by impulsiveness. Frequently we must love by forgiving someone who has not listened for the love we tried to express to him.

TRUE FRIENDSHIP

George Washington

True friendship is a plant of slow growth and must undergo and withstand the shocks of adversity before it is entitled to the appellation.

SAUL, DAVID AND JONATHAN

Saul, as he watched him going out to meet the Philistine, had asked the commander of his men, Abner, from what stock this boy came. On thy life, my lord, said Abner, I cannot tell. So the king bade him find out who the boy's father was; and David fresh from his victory, was taken by Abner into Saul's presence, still carrying the Philistine's head with him. And when Saul asked of his lineage, David told him, I am the son of thy servant Jesse, the Bethlehemite.

By the time he had finished speaking with Saul, David's heart was knit to the heart of Jonathan by a close bond, and Jonathan loved David thenceforward as dearly as his own life. It was then that Saul took David into his service, and would not allow him to go back home; and Jonathan, loving him dearly as his own life, made a covenant of friendship with David, took off his robe and all his gear, even to sword and bow and belt, and gave them David to wear.

Remember, Israel, the dead, wounded on thy heights, the flower of Israel, cut down on thy mountains; how fell they, warriors such as these? Keep the secret in Geth, never a word in the streets of Ascalon; shall the women-folk rejoice, shall they triumph, daughters of the Philistine, the uncircumcised? Mountains of Gelboe, never dew, never rain fall upon you, never from your lands be offering made of first fruits; there the warrior's shield lies dishonoured, the shield of Saul, bright with oil no more. Where the blood of slain men, the flesh of warriors beckoned, never the bow of Jonathan hung back, never the sword of Saul went empty from the feast. Saul and Jonathan, so well beloved, so beautiful; death no more than life could part them; never was eagle so swift, never was lion so strong. Lament, daughters of Israel, lament for Saul, the man who dressed you bravely in scarlet, who decked your apparel out with trinkets of gold. How fell they, warriors such as these, in the battle? On thy heights, Gelboe, Jonathan lies slain. Shall I not mourn for thee, Jonathan my brother, so beautiful, so well beloved, beyond all love of women? Never woman loved her only son, as I thee.

THE FINAL WORD

Dom Moraes

Since I was ten I have not been unkind
To anyone save those who were most close:
Of my close friends one of the best is blind,
One deaf, and one a priest who can't write prose.
None has a quiet mind.

Deep into night my friends with tired faces
Break language up for one word to remain,
The tall forgiving word nothing effaces,
Though without maps it travel, and explain
A pure truth in all places.

TO MY EXCELLENT LUCASTIA
Katherine Philips

Friendship is a delicate plant and can only be grown very seldom for most of us. Acquaintance one can pick up any day, but a friend seems to me almost more of a rarity than a lover; and *he* is rare enough . . . There is another relation between human beings – not friendship and not acquaintanceship either. One may call it perhaps the bond of our common humanity – a firm bond it is too . . . In cities it is felt, I imagine, among the very poor, but the more prosperous you grow the more feeble, as a rule, its hold on you becomes; and perhaps the worst charge one can bring against the commercial era is that it has induced the decadence and virtual disappearance of this bond.

FRIEND
Ralph Wright

You will be my Simon through the years
bearing the burden of my loneliness
from Cyrene
climbing together
against the gravity of price
our Calvary
breaking our toes
against the daily rubble of our falls
and disappointments
you
through every joy and grief
passion or despair
from me
in this before eternity
may God never hide
or in His love
too lastingly or rendingly
divide.

THE PLACE OF THE LION

Charles Williams

After a very few minutes Anthony was compelled to admit that the flat was untenanted. He came back into their common lounge and sat down. Quentin wasn't here; then he was still in flight – or helpless, or dead. The first possibility of the two which had been in Anthony's mind – that of finding his friend – had proved useless; the second and less defined – the hinted discovery in this house of friendship of a means of being of use to the troubled world – remained. He lay back in his chair and let his eyes wander round the room.

The traces of their common occupation lay before him . . . The moments of their past showed themselves multitudinously to him as he looked. Light and amusing, poignant and awful, the different hours of friendship came to him, each full of that suggestion of significance which hours of the kind mysteriously hold – a suggestion which demands definitely either to be accepted as truth or rejected as illusion. Anthony had long since determined on which side his own choice lay; he had accepted those exchanges, so far as mortal frailty could, as being of the nature of final and eternal being. Though they did not last, their importance did; though any friendship might be shattered, no strife and no separation could deny the truth within it: all immortality could but more clearly reveal what in those moments had been . . . He sat on, from recollection passing to reflection, from reflection to obedience, from obedience into a trance of attention. As he had dreamed, if it were a dream, that he rose on powerful wings through the air of the spiritual abyss, so now he felt again the power between Quentin and himself active in its own place. Within that power the presence of his friend grew more defined to him, and the room in which he sat was but the visible extension of an immortal state. He loved; yet not he, but Love living in him. Quentin was surely there, in the room, leaning by the window as he had so often leaned, and Anthony instinctively rose and went across, as he had so often gone across, to join him. If, when he reached it, there was no mortal form, there was yet a reception of him into something that had been and still was; his movement freed it to make a movement of its own . . . His friend. The many moments of joy and deep content which their room had held had in them something of the nature of holy innocence. There had been something in them which was imparted, by Love to love, and which had willed to save them now. Much was possible to a man in solitude; perhaps the final transmutations and achievements in the zones on the yonder side of the central Knowledge were possible only to the spirit in solitude. But some things were possible only to a man in companionship, and of these the most important was balance. No mind was so good that it did not need another mind to counter and equal it, and to save it from conceit and blindness and bigotry and folly. Only in such a balance could humility be found, humility which was a lucid speed to welcome lucidity whenever and wherever it presented itself. How much he owed to Quentin! how much – not pride but delight urged the admission – Quentin owed to him! Balance – and movement in balance, as an eagle sails up on the wind – this was the truth of life, and beauty in life.

Bibliography

BIBLIOGRAPHY

Abhishiktananda. *Prayer.* SPCK

Ashford, Daisy. *The Young Visiters.* Chatto, 1957

Belloc, Hilaire. *Sonnets and Verse.* Duckworth, 1954

Boros, Ladislaus. *In Time of Temptation.* Search Press, 1968

Boulding, Maria. *A Touch of God.* SPCK, 1982

Brahms, C. and Simon, S. J. *A Mutual Pair.* Michael Joseph, 1976

Brooke, Rupert. *1914 and Other Poems.* Sidgwick and Jackson, 1915

Buber, Martin. *Between Man and Man.* Fontana, 1961

Camus, Albert. *Lyrical and Critical.* Hamish Hamilton, 1967

Carter, Sydney. *The Rock of Doubt.* Mowbray, 1978

Caussade, J. P. de. *Self-Abandonment to Divine Providence,* Burns & Oates

Chardin, Pierre Teilhard de. *The Making of a Mind.* Collins, 1965

Chesterton, G. K. *The Napoleon of Notting Hill.* Bodley Head, 1904

Cloud of Unknowing, The. Anon

Coffin, Charles M. (ed). *The Major Poets.* Harcourt, USA, 1954

Craig, Mary. *Blessings.* Hodder, 1979

Candles in the Dark. Hodder, 1984

Cummings, E. E. *The Complete Poems 1913-62.* Granada

Dalrymple, John. *Costing Not Less Than Everything.* Darton, Longman and Todd, 1975

Donleavy, J. P. *The Beastly Beatitudes of Balthazar B.* Penguin, 1970

Doonican, Val. *The Special Years.* Elm Tree Books, 1980

Dostoevsky, F. M. *The Brothers Karamazov.* Penguin, 1970

Duncan, Anthony. *The Lord of the Dance.* Helios, 1972

Dunsany, Lord. *The King of Elfland's Daughter.* Unwin Paperbacks, 1982

Flaubert, Gustave. *Madame Bovary.* Penguin, 1970

Frankl, Viktor E. *Man's Search for Meaning.* Hodder, 1963

French, R. M. *The Way of a Pilgrim* (translation). SPCK, 1972

Fynn. *Mister God, This is Anna.* Fontana, 1977

Gallico, Paul. *The Lonely.* Michael Joseph, 1954

The Snow Goose. Michael Joseph, 1969

Gardner, Helen. *The Metaphysical Poets.* Penguin, 1969

Gibran, Kahlil. *The Prophet.* Heinemann, 1972

Grahame, Kenneth. *The Wind in the Willows.* Methuen, 1971

Graves, Robert. *Selected by Himself.* Penguin, 1957

Grenfell, Joyce. *In Pleasant Places.* Macmillan, 1979

Guinness, Bryan. *Collected Poems.* Heinemann, 1956

Hadfield, John (ed). *A Book of Love.* Boydell Press, 1980

Hamilton, Edith. *Mythology.* Mentor Books

Hamilton, Elizabeth. *Heloise.* Hodder, 1966

Hammarskjold, Dag. *Markings.* Faber, 1964

Hardy, Thomas. *Far from the Madding Crowd.* Pan, 1978

Heaney, Seamus and Hughes, Ted. *The Rattle Bag.* Faber, 1982

Iremonger, Valentine. *Horan's Field.* Dolmen Press, Dublin, 1972

Jacob, Violet. *Songs of Angus.* John Murray

Johnston, William. *Silent Music: Way to Meditation.* Fontana, 1976

Jung, C. G. *Psychological Reflections.* Routledge, 1971

Kipling, Rudyard. *The Definitive Edition of Rudyard Kipling's Verse.* Hodder, 1940

Lessing, Doris. *Collected African Stories,* Vol 1. Panther, 1979

Lewis, Alun. *In the Green Tree.* George Allen & Unwin

Lewis, C. S. *The Four Loves.* Fontana, 1963

A Grief Observed. Faber, 1966

Surprised by Joy. Fontana, 1959

Voyage to Venus. Pan, 1968

The Allegory of Love. OUP, 1968

Lewis, D. B. Wyndham and Searle, Ronald. *The Terror of St. Trinian's.* I. Henry Publications, 1976

Lusseyran, Jacques. *The Blind in Society.* Myrin Institute for Adult Education, USA, 1973

MacDonald, George. *At the Back of the North Wind.* Scripture Union, 1978

Malory, Sir Thomas. *Le Morte D'Arthur.* Dent, 1906

McGinley, Phyllis. *Times Three.* Viking Press, USA, 1960

Maritain, Jacques. *Creative Intuition in Art and Poetry.* Meridian Books, USA, 1968

Menuhin, Yehudi. *Unfinished Journey.* Futura, 1978

Meredith, George. *The Ordeal of Richard Feverel.* Dent, 1935

Merton, Thomas. *The Sign of Jonas.* Sheldon Press, 1976

Moncrieff, George Scott. *Burke Street.* Richard Patterson, 1956

Montague, John. *Irish Verse.* Faber, 1974

Moore, Geoffrey (ed). *The Penguin Book of American Verse.* Penguin, 1977

Morgan, Edwin. *Poems of Thirty Years.* Carcanet Press, 1982

Muggeridge, Malcolm. *The Green Stick.* Fontana, 1975

Muir, Edwin. *The Collected Poems of Edwin Muir.* Faber, 1963

Murdoch, Iris. *The Black Prince.* Penguin, 1975

Nash, Ogden. *I Wouldn't Have Missed It.* André Deutsch, 1983

Newman, Nanette. *God Bless Love.* Collins, 1972

O'Brien, Flann. *The Best of Myles.* Pan, 1977

O'Flaherty, Liam. *More Short Stories of Liam O'Flaherty.* Cape, 1937

Orage, A. R. *On Love.* Samuel Weiser Inc., USA, 1974

Palgrave, Francis. *The Golden Treasury.* Collins, 1973

Peake, Mervyn. *Mister Pye.* Penguin, 1972

Poems of Today: An Anthology. Published for English Association. Sidgwick and Jackson, 1915

Post, Laurens van der. *The Lost World of the Kalahari.* Penguin, 1964

Venture to the Interior. Penguin, 1971

Potts, Paul. *Dante Called You Beatrice.* Eyre and Spottiswoode, 1961

Powell, Claire. *The Meaning of Flowers.* Jupiter Books, 1977

Rahner, Hugo. *Man at Play.* Burns & Oates, 1972

Rahner, Karl. *The Eternal Year,* Dimension Books, USA, 1980

Raine, Kathleen. *Collected Poems.* Hamish Hamilton, 1956

Saint-Exupery, Antoine de. *The Little Prince.* Pan, 1982

Samaan-Hanna, A. *Moods That Endure.* Stanbrook Abbey Press, 1979

Selig, Richard. *Poems.* Dolmen Press, Dublin, 1962

Silcock, Arnold. *Verse and Worse.* Faber, 1971

Silkin, Jon. *Selected Poems.* Routledge & Kegan Paul, 1980

Sitwell, Edith. *Collected Poems.* Macmillan, 1957

Spender, Stephen. *Collected Poems.* Faber, 1955

Stallworthy, Jon. *Root and Branch.* Chatto & Windus, 1976

Stassinopoulos, Arianna. *Maria: Beyond the Callas Legend.* Weidenfeld, 1980

Steinbeck, John. *Tortilla Flat.* Pan, 1975

The Winter of Our Discontent. Pan, 1970

Stephens, James. *Desire.* Poolbeg Press, Dublin, 1980

Stevenson, Sir John and Bishop, Sir Henry. *More Irish Melodies.* Gill, Dublin, 1885

Synge, J. M. *Plays.* OUP, 1968

Tagore, Rabindranath. *The Collected Poems and Plays of Rabindranath Tagore.* Macmillan, 1936

Termier, P. *La Joie de Connaître.*

Thomas, Dylan. *Selected Works.* Book Club Associates, 1976

Thomas, R. S. *Song at the Year's Turning.* Hart-Davis, 1955

Thornton, Robert D. (ed). *The Tuneful Flame: Songs of Robert Burns as He Sang Them.* University of Kansas Press, USA, 1957

Thurber, James. *The Thirteen Clocks and The Wonderful O.* Penguin, 1970

Tolkien, J. R. R. *The Fellowship of the Ring.* Unwin Paperbacks, 1981

Vanauken, Sheldon. *A Severe Mercy.* Hodder, 1977

Watts, Alan W. *Nature, Man and Woman.* Abacus, 1976

Weil, Simone. *Gateway to God.* Fontana, 1974

West, Morris. *Harlequin.* Fontana, 1976

White, Patrick. *Riders in the Chariot.* Penguin, 1964

White, T. H. *The Once and Future King.* Fontana, 1969

Whitehead, A. N. *Science and The Modern World*

Wilde, Oscar. *The Importance of Being Earnest.* Eyre Methuen, 1975

Wilder, Thornton. *The Bridge of San Luis Rey.* Penguin, 1969

Williams, Charles. *The Place of the Lion.* Eerdmans, USA, 1933

Williams, Margery. *The Velveteen Rabbit.* Heinemann, 1970

Williams, Oscar (ed). *The Pocket Book of Modern Verse.* Pocket Books Inc., USA, 1958

Williams, W. E. *Browning (A Selection).* Penguin, 1954

Williamson, Henry. *Goodbye to the West Country.* Macdonald

Wood, Denis. *Poets in the Garden.* John Murray, 1978

Wurmbrand, Richard. *In God's Underground.* W. H. Allen, 1968

Yeats, W. B. *Collected Poems.* Macmillan, 1950

Acknowledgments

ACKNOWLEDGMENTS

The author and publisher have endeavoured to trace all copyright holders for the material in this anthology but apologise for any inadvertent omissions which will be rectified in any reprint.

Abhishiktananda, 'Prayer', is reprinted by permission of SPCK.

Daisy Ashford, *The Young Visiters*, is reprinted by permission of the Author's Estate and Chatto & Windus.

Hilaire Belloc, 'From Quiet Homes' and 'Juliet', from *Sonnets and Verse* published by Gerald Duckworth & Sons Ltd., is reprinted by permission of A. D. Peters & Co.

Maria Boulding, *A Touch of God*, is reprinted by permission of SPCK.

C. Brahms and S. J. Simon, *A Mutual Pair*, published by Michael Joseph, is reprinted by permission of Curtis Brown Ltd.

Martin Buber, *Between Man and Man*, is reprinted by permission of Routledge & Kegan Paul.

Gerald Bullett, 'The Lover Bids His Heart Be Absent', is reprinted by permission of A. D. Peters & Co.

Albert Camus, extracts from *Lyrical and Critical*, translated by P. Thody, is reprinted by permission of Hamish Hamilton Ltd.

John Carey, review, 'Uncollected Poems by John Betjeman', is reprinted by permission of Times Newspapers Ltd.

Sydney Carter, *The Rock of Doubt*, is reprinted by permission of A. R. Mowbray & Co. Ltd.

J. P. de Caussade, *Self-Abandonment to Divine Providence*, is reprinted by permission of Burns & Oates Ltd.

Pierre Teilhard de Chardin, *The Making of a Mind*, is reprinted by permission of William Collins Ltd.

G. K. Chesterton, *The Napoleon of Notting Hill*, is reprinted by permission of The Bodley Head Ltd.

Noël Coward, 'Loving', is reprinted by permission of Michael Imison Playwrights Ltd.

Mary Craig, *Blessings* and *Candles in the Dark*, is reprinted by permission of Hodder & Stoughton Ltd.

E. E. Cummings, 'Love is a Place', from *The Complete Poems 1913-1962* by E. E. Cummings, is reprinted by permission of Granada Publishing Ltd.

Fr. John Dalrymple, *Costing Not Less Than Everything*, published and copyright 1978 by Darton, Longman and Todd, is used by permission of the publishers.

Walter de la Mare, 'Music', is reprinted by permission of the Literary Trustees of Walter de la Mare and The Society of Authors as their Representative.

J. P. Donleavy, *The Beastly Beatitudes of Balthazar B*, is reprinted by kind permission of the author and Penguin Books.

Val Doonican, *The Special Years*, published by Elm Tree Books, is reprinted by permission of Hamish Hamilton Ltd.

Lord Dunsany, 'Helen of Troy', is reprinted by kind permission of Curtis Brown Ltd. on behalf of John Child Villiers and Valentine Lamb as literary executors of Lord Dunsany. Copyright Estate of Lord Dunsany.

Lord Dunsany, *The King of Elfland's Daughter*, is reprinted by permission of George Allen & Unwin.

Eleanor Farjeon, 'Soldier', is reprinted by permission of David Higham Associates.

Viktor E. Frankl, *Man's Search for Meaning*, is reprinted by permission of Hodder & Stoughton Ltd, and Beacon Press.

R. M. French, *The Way of the Pilgrim*, is reprinted by permission of SPCK.

Fynn, *Mister God, This Is Anna*, is reprinted by permission of William Collins Ltd.

Paul Gallico, *The Lonely* and *The Snow Goose*, published by Michael Joseph, is reprinted by permission of Hughes Massie Ltd.

Kahlil Gibran, *The Prophet*, published by William Heinemann Ltd., 1972, is reprinted by permission of Alfred A. Knopf, Inc.

Randy Goodrum, 'You Needed Me', is reprinted by permission of Chappell & Co., Inc.

Robert Graves, 'One Hard Look' and 'At First Sight', from *Collected Poems 1975*, is reprinted by permission of Robert Graves.

Joyce Grenfell, *In Pleasant Places*, is reprinted by permission of Macmillan Ltd., London and Basingstoke.

Bryan Guinness, 'By Loch Etive', from *Collected Poems*, published by William Heinemann Ltd., 1956, is reprinted by kind permission of Lord Moyne.

Edith Hamilton, *Mythology*, is reprinted by permission of Little Brown & Co., Boston.

Elizabeth Hamilton, *Heloise*, copyright Elizabeth Hamilton 1966, is reprinted by permission of Curtis Brown Ltd.

Dag Hammarskjold, 'Thou Takest the Pen', from *Markings*, is reprinted by permission of Faber and Faber.

Violet Jacob, 'Tam i' The Kirk', from *Songs of Angus,* is reprinted by permission of John Murray (Publishers) Ltd.

Pat Johnson, 'Floral Symphony', copyright © Pat Johnson, is reprinted by permission of the author.

W. Johnston, *Silent Music,* is reprinted by permission of William Collins Ltd.

C. Jung, *Psychological Reflections,* is reprinted by permission of Routledge & Kegan Paul.

Rudyard Kipling, 'L'Envoi', 'In Springtime' and 'Sussex', from *The Definitive Edition of Rudyard Kipling's Verse,* are reprinted by permission of The National Trust for Places of Historic or Natural Beauty and Macmillan London Ltd.

Jeannette Kupfermann, article, 'Mr and Mrs Sharansky', *Sunday Times* 5/2/84, is reprinted by kind permission of Jeannette Kupferman.

Doris Lessing, 'The Antheap', from *Five,* © 1953 Doris Lessing, is reprinted by permission of Jonathan Clowes Ltd. on behalf of Doris Lessing.

Bernard Levin, 'Enthusiasms', is reprinted by kind permission of Bernard Levin.

Alun Lewis, 'Postscript for Gwen', from *In the Green Tree,* is reprinted by permission of George Allen & Unwin.

C. S. Lewis, *A Grief Observed,* is reprinted by permission of Faber and Faber Ltd. *Surprised by Joy* and *The Four Loves* are reprinted by permission of William Collins Ltd.

D. B. Wyndham Lewis and Ronald Searle, *The Terror of St. Trinian's,* is reprinted by permission of A. D. Peters & Co. Ltd.

Jacques Lusseyran, *The Blind in Society,* © 1973 by the Myrin Institute, is reprinted by permission of the Myrin Institute.

A. M. Mackenzie, 'Island Moon', is reprinted by kind permission of J. & W. Chester. Edition Wilhelm Hansen London Ltd.

John Masefield, 'Sea Fever' and 'Twilight', are reprinted by permission of The Society of Authors as literary representative of the Estate of John Masefield.

Phyllis McGinley, 'Launcelot with Bicycle', from *Times Three* by Phyllis McGinley, copyright © 1960 by Phyllis McGinley, is reprinted by permission of Viking Penguin, Inc., New York.

Yehudi Menuhin, *Unfinished Journey,* is reprinted by permission of Macdonald & Co. (Publishers) Ltd.

Thomas Merton, *The Sign of Jonas,* is reprinted by permission of Harcourt Brace Jovanovich, Inc., and Sheldon Press.

Edwin Morgan, 'Strawberries', © Edwin Morgan, from *Poems of Thirty Years,* Carcanet Press, Manchester, 1982, is reprinted by permission of the publishers.

Malcolm Muggeridge, *The Green Stick,* is reprinted by permission of William Collins Ltd. Extracts from *Chronicles of Wasted Time* and *What I Believe* are reprinted by kind permission of the author.

Edwin Muir, 'The Confirmation', from *The Collected Poems of Edwin Muir,* is reprinted by permission of Faber and Faber Ltd.

Iris Murdoch, *The Black Prince,* is reprinted by permission of Chatto & Windus.

Ogden Nash, 'Song to be Sung by the Father of Infant Female Children', from *I Wouldn't Have Missed It,* published by André Deutsch, 1983, is reprinted by permission of André Deutsch.

Nanette Newman (ed), *God Bless Love,* is reprinted by permission of William Collins Ltd.

Flann O'Brien, *The Best of Myles,* is reprinted by permission of Granada Publishing Ltd.

Mervyn Peake, *Mister Pye,* published by Penguin, 1972, is reprinted by permission of David Higham Associates Ltd.

William Plomer, 'Dragon-Fly Love', is reprinted by kind permission of Rupert Hart-Davis and the Executors of the William Plomer Estate.

Laurens van der Post, *The Lost World of the Kalahari* and *Venture to the Interior,* is reprinted by permission of The Hogarth Press.

Claire Powell, *The Meaning of Flowers,* is reprinted by permission of Jupiter Books.

Karl Rahner, *The Eternal Year,* is reprinted by permission of Burns & Oates Ltd.

Kathleen Raine, 'Spell of Creation', from *Collected Poems* is reprinted by permission of George Allen & Unwin.

Antoine de Saint-Exupery, *The Little Prince,* is reprinted by permission of William Heinemann Ltd.

A. Samaan-Hanna, extracts from *Moods that Endure,* published by Stanbrook Abbey Press, is reprinted by permission of the author.

Siegfried Sassoon, 'Everyone Sang', is reprinted by permission of George Sassoon.

Franz Schubert, 'An die Musik', translation, is reprinted by permission of Decca International.

Jon Silkin, 'Caring for Animals' and 'A Space in the Air', from *Selected Poems* by Jon Silkin, published by Routledge & Kegan Paul, is reprinted by permission of Routledge & Kegan Paul.

Edith Sitwell, 'Said the Sun to the Moon', from

Photographs